S0-EDL-081

Paper
Best wishes
Den

Solve for the Customer

SOLVE FOR THE CUSTOMER

Using Customer Science to Build Stronger Relationships and Improve Business Results

By Denis Pombriant

Copyright © Denis R. Pombriant 2015
All rights reserved.

This book is published by PawPrints, a division of Beagle Research Group, LLC.

All rights reserved. No part of this publication may be reproduced, stored in a retrieval system or transmitted in any form, or by any means, electronic, mechanical, photocopying, recording, scanning, or otherwise, except as permitted under Section 107 or 108 of the 1976 United States Copyright Act, without the prior written permission of the author.

Limit of Liability/Disclaimer of Warranty: While the publisher and author have used their best efforts in preparing this book, they make no representations or warranties with the respect to the accuracy or completeness of the contents of this book and specifically disclaim any implied warranties of merchantability or fitness for a particular purpose. No warranty may be created or extended by sales representatives or written sales materials. The advice and strategies contained herein may not be suitable for your situation. You should consult with a professional where appropriate. Neither the publisher nor the author shall be liable for damages arising herefrom.

Information about Beagle Research Group or Denis Pombriant

Twitter: @DenisPombriant

Facebook: Denis Pombriant

LinkedIn: Denis Pombriant

Email: Denis@BeagleResearch.com

Website: BeagleResearch.com

Telephone: 781-297-0066; 415-287-0427

ISBN-13: 978-1502387813
ISBN-10: 1502387816

Copyright © 2015 by Denis R. Pombriant

Once again for Kathy, Alec, and Jack.

About the Author

Denis Pombriant is an analyst in the CRM market and founder and managing principal of Beagle Research Group, LLC. He is a researcher, speaker, consultant, and a frequent contributor to *CRM* magazine, destinationCRM.com, CRMBuyer.com, and other publications in the CRM space. He is also a long time member of the Enterprise Irregulars and he has been a primary judge in the CRM Idol competition. Since 2000 he has been a leader in uncovering and writing about emerging CRM issues, including the growing importance of SaaS, social media, mobility, and analytics. His first book, *Hello, Ladies: Dispatches from the Social CRM Frontier* (2010) compiled his writings about CRM's early days in social media. Popular Beagle Research reports include *The InterBoom* (2010), which examines how CRM could help spur business in a down economy, and *The New Garage* (2004), which predicted the rise of platform technology in the front office. Pombriant has a B.A. from The College of the Holy Cross and lives in the Boston area.

Contents

ABOUT THE AUTHOR...VI

FOREWORD VIII

INTRODUCTION 1

   CHAPTER ONE...3
      YOUR CUSTOMERS HATE YOU (OKAY, *SOME* OF THEM)

   CHAPTER TWO 19
      OLD BUSINESS MODELS CONTRIBUTE TO THE PROBLEM

   CHAPTER THREE 36
      THE POWER OF THE SUBSCRIPTION MODEL

   CHAPTER FOUR...50
      THE ANNA KARENINA PRINCIPLE AND MOMENTS OF TRUTH

   CHAPTER FIVE...68
      USE GOOD JUDGMENT

   CHAPTER SIX 86
      GATHERING CUSTOMER DATA THROUGH COMMUNITY

   CHAPTER SEVEN..106
      TYPES OF COMMUNITIES; THE SYMANTEC STORY

   CHAPTER EIGHT...119
      A MANAGED COMMUNITY: HP SOFTWARE'S BIG DATA BUSINESS UNIT
      AND GET SATISFACTION

   CHAPTER NINE...141
      COMMUNISPACE: A MEDIATED COMMUNITY

   CHAPTER TEN 150
      THE FUTURE OF COMMUNITY

   CHAPTER ELEVEN...162
      CUSTOMER SCIENCE

ENDNOTES..173

ACKNOWLEDGEMENTS...178

Foreword

I've been in the CRM industry for almost two decades and have watched it grow from a small industry to what has become a near-ubiquitous technological and systemic requirement for businesses. Countless companies worldwide now use software to create systems for sales, marketing, and customer service. But technology alone is not enough, never was. People and process elements need to be re-thought.

Think about this: In the past decade we have undergone a communication revolution that has impacted every person and every institution on the planet. How we communicate — with each other, with institutions — has permanently changed. There are almost 7 billion mobile devices on the planet, of which 2.4 billon are smart devices. The devices we use, the expectations of the communication we have, and the time within which we expect responses have all dramatically altered to favor better communication.

In addition, our means and expectations of communication have transformed how we create, distribute, and consume information. We now have the ability to instantly get the information we are looking for in a format that we can read, hear, or see, at the time we want it, wherever we are.

For business this means that customers have the upper hand. For the first time in business history customers control the conversation about a brand. The brand information that they need is available in a structured way at their fingertips and in an unstructured way (from user reviews of products or services to conversations on how to do something with those products and users), as long as customers have the tools to access it — usually, a search engine will do.

Most important, 21st-century customers are entitled. They aren't looking for what you can do for them as the sole criterion for purchase; they also look at how they feel about you over time. They want a positive experience in a long-standing engagement that is personalized to their needs. This means you have to know not only the demographics of a customer segment, but also the individual information that gives you the insight to formulate a conversation — even if some of it is automated — that feels personal with a particular customer. The customer has to feel valued, which requires you to have insight about that customer. If you are a large business and scale to millions of customers, you understand how daunting a task this can be. That's what makes *Solve for the Customer*, Denis Pombriant's insights into Customer Science, so interesting.

I've known Denis for more than half of my sojourn in the CRM industry. He's not only a great friend, but is also one of the most important voices that the business world has. Denis's unique blend of business, sociological, behavioral, technological, scientific, economic, political, and cultural smarts is a rare combination that provides him with an outlook that few others have, not just on the state of the world, but also on how to deal with particular aspects of it — especially the transformed customer.

This is why this world of ours needs a Denis Pombriant. Hell, we need *this* Denis Pombriant. We need Denis to explain to us his idea of Customer Science — and in this book, he does just that.

Solve for the Customer does something that has been sorely needed in the business world for a long time: It gives us a blueprint for how we can figure out not just what customers want from our businesses, but also how to execute. For many years we have been making what are at best educated guesses at how to provide customers what they want. But with socioeconomic factors influencing customers' demands and desires more than at any time in the past, we have to combine the art of customer engagement with science so that we have the complete customer-oriented package.

Solve for the Customer provides the missing piece — the science. That means both the social science — the cultures and behaviors that define customers — and the methodology to accomplish those things that bring value to both the business and the customer.

What makes this particularly cogent is that we are at a point in history where what customers value and what businesses value are two very different things. On the one hand, businesses value profitability, revenue, shareholder value, and customer satisfaction — things that you easily can measure. On the other hand, customers value being *valued*. It's a feeling, not a mathematical construct. As Denis writes in *Solve for the Customer*, vendors seek transactions, customers value process, and attention to process is how vendors can value customers.

But businesses have a dilemma: Even though they have to do the things that make customers feel valued, businesses need to figure out how valuable customers are to *them*. In the past that was measured via customer lifetime value, how much customers are worth to the business in purchasing power over their transactional life with the company. And now, the proliferation of new forms of communication and new ways to consume information makes this much more complex. The customer provides value to the company through referrals, through brand influence, and through content creation relative to the brand. The issue is not only direct impact on revenue through transactions, but also indirect impact on revenue through interaction.

A business has to figure out how to do the things that allow it to provide measurable value to customers so that it can have an accurate idea of the costs and the benefits to the business of that value provision. To even get to the point that this matters, there have to be effective programs, strategies, processes, business rules, technologies, and systems that can make all this happen.

Solve for the Customer solves all this for both customers and the businesses that are trying to understand how to do it. Denis brings us this in one place. It is enormously valuable. Finally, in that one place, is a scientifically valid approach to dealing with customers, giving them what they need within the constraints of your business, and getting the optimal value from those very same individuals. This is something that Denis Pombriant does. And so, he does it again.

Paul Greenberg, February 2015

Introduction

There is a great divide between vendors and customers that has withstood multiple attempts to bring the two sides together. Think of the aphorism[1] about England and America being two countries separated by a common language: Vendors and customers coexist and deal with occasional misunderstanding or worse, even after vendors implement customer relationship management (CRM) software. Vendors want and need commerce and profits, so they cast broad nets for customers and watch for any opportunity to reduce costs. Customers understand this, but they want and need products and services, which often extend to things beyond the basic article to include after-sale service, advice, training, and much more — what organizational theorists Regis McKenna, Geoffrey Moore, and others have called *whole product*. Vendors are learning this but their business systems have not kept up with market demands.

The Internet's emergence has often accentuated vendor-customer differences, rather than bringing the sides together. Customers have never had as much power to announce their displeasure with vendors and to influence other customers' opinions as they do now through social media, and vendors have never had such an easy time of sending offers — welcome or not — to customers through nearly free Internet services. But the two sides still talk past each other.

Until recently the vendor-customer relationship has been a haphazard affair, based on random acts of CRM and/or hunches that businesses use to try to penetrate their markets. Market analysis has been a static thing for the most part, one and done, and vendors' approaches to their markets have hardly changed for a long time.

But a change is coming. Big data and analytics have delivered important tools that not only give vendors and customers better ways to understand each other, but also have spawned a new science of the customer, or more formally, Customer Science.

Leading companies are rapidly progressing from these random acts of CRM to Customer Science, a social science that operates on the graceful functions of the bell curve rather than the abstruse equations of physics. Data gathering and analytics are producing bodies of evidence specific to each business that give managers and executives the confidence they need to pursue actions that at first blush may seem counterintuitive, but which in fact offer nuggets of insight.

Customer Science must be practiced by people employing modern technologies within defined business processes — the people, process, and technology mantra that we've heard so often. The need for Customer Science is abundantly clear. All you have to do is scan the Internet to find customer testimonials and negative sentiment about how vendors have failed to provide the essentials in their customer relationships.

Perhaps our reliance on pure technological approaches at the expense of inserting people into customer-facing business processes has contributed to the failure. Customer Science offers approaches that enable vendors to maintain the benefits of automation in ways that support better processes, mediated, when needed, by people dedicated to improving relationships.

Solve for the Customer introduces logical ways to capture and process customer data that enable vendors to be more in the moment with their customers. It also suggests that changing the perspective of customer experience from a *noun* (i.e., the customer experience) to a *verb,* or how a customer experiences a product, a process, or an interaction with a vendor, can have a dramatic impact on customer bonding and advocacy — the essentials for vendor success in today's marketplace.

Customer Science is now a necessity because so many customers are so dissatisfied — and they are not timid about telling the world why. This is a business problem and much can be done to solve it. We have to start by asking why so many customers hate their vendors.

Chapter One

Your Customers Hate You (Okay, *Some* of Them)

Below a March 27, 2013, *New York Times* headline that read, "Court Rejects Antitrust Suit in Victory for Comcast," reporter Edward Wyatt wrote that the U.S. Supreme Court had thrown out a proposed class-action lawsuit by a group of more than two million Comcast cable subscribers. According to the article, "The plaintiffs accused Comcast of creating a monopoly by buying cable groups in the Philadelphia area that gave it 69 percent of that market in 2007, up from 24 percent in 1998."[1] The subscribers were suing for $875 million in damages. Put simply, the suit alleged that Comcast had created a monopoly so that it could raise prices; the present and former customers wanted some of their money back.

Comcast's tactics, which were well documented in Susan P. Crawford's excellent book, *Captive Audience: The Telecom Industry and Monopoly Power in the New Gilded Age,*[2] are relatively common in the cable industry, where providers engage in what Crawford calls clustering: trading service areas so that each provider ends up with contiguous territory to make it easier to string cables and service their respective customer bases — all without competition.

The practice also affects traditional telecommunications providers, since cable and phone services have been seeping into each other's businesses for many years. Through clustering, cable companies could more or less select their customers and reduce the cost of providing service, something that telecommunications providers couldn't do. Telecoms had to take all comers according to rules put in place by the Federal Communications Commission (FCC) — rules that mysteriously don't apply to cable.

Clustering tactics aren't new, though the underlying technologies may be. Railroads tried a version of this approach in the 19th century, and just about any new service that requires a heavy investment in infrastructure is prone to it.[3] The way to make a profit in an infrastructure-intensive business is to minimize the necessary infrastructure while using it to serve the greatest number of customers. The more people you can serve, the more profitable you can be. That's why heavily populated urban areas get new infrastructure first and rural areas always seem to be the last to get things like electricity, telephone, and cable.

To an untrained eye, the class-action suit seemed to have merit and it was odd to see the Supreme Court take on such a case. But too often in the run up to a court date, attorneys play a game of inside baseball, perfectly legal, in which they attempt to prevent a trial by discrediting their opponent's case in pretrial motions. Comcast's legal maneuvering involved questioning whether or not the two million angry subscribers were, in fact, a class that was homogeneous enough to sue under the rules of class actions. A federal appeals court had already decided this point in favor of the plaintiffs, ruling that they were indeed a class; the issue ended up before the high court after Comcast appealed. So, from the Supreme Court's perspective, the case turned on the narrow definition of a class — not on the merits of the class's claims against Comcast. The majority, in an opinion written by Justice Antonin Scalia, said no, they weren't a class, and threw the case out in a 5-to-4 decision.

A 5-to-4 majority is as thin as it gets, but it's enough to win an argument in this democracy. The minority, though, was as aggrieved (they don't get mad on the Supreme Court) as a cat dropped in a toilet by a two-year-old.

The minority quartet, led by Justice Ruth Bader Ginsburg, wrote in its dissent that the majority had produced a ruling that "...is good for this day and case only," and "...sets forth a profoundly mistaken view of antitrust law."[4] You could interpret this as the minority accusing the majority of being the bagman for Comcast.

But as Supreme Court Justice Robert H. Jackson wrote in 1953, "We are not final because we are infallible, but we are infallible only because we are final."[5]

Such is life in big-time law.

In a statement that rounded everything out, Comcast said: "We are pleased that the Supreme Court found that a class should not have been certified in this case."

You bet Comcast was pleased.

So, as the old Miller Brewing Company ad declared, "It's it. And that's that." Or is it? Comcast got two million customers mad enough to join a class-action suit — and that was just in Philadelphia. The question needs to be asked: How can Comcast or any major company (short of a monopoly), create so many angry customers and yet, stay in business? Answering that question — and showing how to avoid similar situations in the future — is what *Solve for the Customer* is about.

But hang on, there's more.

Standoff — United Breaks Guitars

The legal system may have deprived all those Comcast subscribers of the chance to pursue their class-action suit, but this is not the only way to lose a fight when confronting a large corporation. In fact, you can even lose when it looks like you've won.

Nobody won in the infamous United Breaks Guitars mess, for example — not if *winning* means affecting some kind of change or effecting a satisfactory resolution. United Breaks Guitars turned into a classic case of rope-a-dope: one combatant expending energy to no avail, oblivious to the pain and the cost of the standoff. In case you're one of the few people on the planet not to have seen the videos or heard the songs, let's recap.

The Sons of Maxwell, a group of Canadian musicians, were traveling from their home base in Halifax, Nova Scotia, to play a gig near Omaha, NE. The group's itinerary on United Airlines routed them through Chicago's O'Hare International Airport, where they (and their luggage, including their instruments) were to change planes. While waiting to deplane in Chicago, the band's leader, Dave Carroll, heard another passenger say that the luggage handlers were "throwing guitars." On arrival in Omaha, Carroll found that his $3,500 Taylor guitar had been severely damaged in transit, but he was unable to file a claim until he returned home. Thus began Carroll's yearlong odyssey through the labyrinth of United's customer-service system in a vain attempt to recoup the cost of repairing the instrument.

United denied Carroll's initial claim, falling back on its rules for filing complaints, and effectively stonewalled Carroll thereafter. After nine months of runaround, Carroll took his case public in an effort to shame the airline into acknowledging his claim's legitimacy. Carroll's campaign included writing songs and posting YouTube videos documenting his efforts.

Carroll posted the first "United Breaks Guitars" video[6] with the original song to YouTube on July 6, 2009, and it spread like chickenpox in an elementary school. Within one day the video received 150,000 views, finally prompting United to move to accept responsibility and attempt to right the situation — but the airline's efforts came too late. United suffered a public relations disaster and took a major hit to its brand.

And the situation only got worse.

The original video amassed more than a half-million views in just three days, and five million views by mid-August. And the hits just kept on coming. Carroll released a second song on YouTube on August 17, 2009, taking aim at United's policies and business practices. He released his trilogy's final song, "United We Stand,"[7] in March 2010, attempting to put things into perspective by saying that United employees are not "all bad apples," but are forced to uphold policies that are simply outdated if not completely wrong.

Carroll got a lot of publicity for his efforts and a new career as a public speaker on the topic of customer service. In December 2009, *Time* magazine ranked "United Breaks Guitars" number seven in its list of the year's Top 10 Viral Videos. Carroll also published a book, *United Breaks Guitars: The Power of One Voice in the Age of Social Media*.[8]

Power?

Carroll may have declared victory, but his shaming strategy ultimately failed despite his book's spin on the incident and its topical references to social media. No one won much of anything in this dispute, and both sides suffered losses. United's brand was shredded for its ineptitude and Carroll was never directly compensated by the airline for his loss. Instead, United donated $3,000 to the Thelonious Monk Institute of Jazz.

It was a Pyrrhic victory for Carroll at best, and it's hard to see how his approach to getting a corporation to pay adequate attention to customer concerns can scale. Public shaming is not a long-term strategy, as we'll see. The public has a short attention span and a low tolerance for repetition. The United Breaks Guitars event was a novelty and it got the Warholian 15 minutes of fame it deserved. It's doubtful that a future Dave Carroll would be so lucky. If everyone with a gripe against a corporation took Carroll's approach, complaints would be so numerous they would drown each other out. People were entertained by the episode for a while, and United's stock price took a brief hit, but people still fly the carrier, bound like barnacles through frequent-flier miles.

It's worth noting that even before the incident United was not a financially healthy company. The airline was cutting costs, and would merge with Continental Airlines in 2010. A broken guitar was barely a blip on its radar. From my research, many people still have numerous gripes with this airline and the industry in general, but things don't change much: People keep flying carriers they dislike. As we'll see in the coming chapters, frequent-flier programs and similar customer-loyalty efforts work almost as well as a monopoly for hanging on to unhappy customers.

The cost of trying

Comcast got what it wanted, at least in the short run, but its two million present-and-former customers got nothing. Nor did the law firm handling the plaintiffs' case, which must have hurt because class actions are go-for-broke propositions. The attorneys don't get paid unless there is a judgment in favor of the plaintiffs, because the plaintiffs can't pay a legal bill that could easily reach six or seven figures.

Class actions bring together a large number of people who allegedly have been harmed, for example, by a business practice, and yet in many (but not all) situations they've been harmed relatively little. It would thus make no sense for the people to sue the vendor individually, because the costs of litigation would be so much higher than that of whatever compensation might be recovered. That's why nothing typically happens unless a group or class can, in legal parlance, be formed or certified. The Supreme Court said there was no class in the Comcast situation; by extension, there could be no suit.

One of the hallmarks of American justice is that every person can have a day in court — provided the person can afford to hire lawyers and be patient enough to wait for the process to unwind. Very often we resort to lawsuits against vendors when nothing else seems to get their attention, but sometimes we sue before we've exhausted all other possibilities — perhaps because we're angry. As a proverb says, however, the first one to get angry loses the argument.

A primary point of *Solve for the Customer* is that there are now more possible ways to get big corporations to pay attention to customers than there ever have been. These possibilities don't involve courtrooms or public shaming, and I believe that many of these alternatives might work better than legal plays. More than that, if recent court decisions like the Comcast case serve as guides, the courts and the American public may be growing weary of class-action suits. So if the objective is resolution, not retribution, new technologies aimed at helping vendors and customers to understand each other better — technologies that head off disagreements before they have a chance to form — may be just what the doctor, or in this case the court, indirectly, ordered.

Monopoly power

There's a dynamic tension between vendors and customers that's as old and as fundamental as selling and buying. It costs money to compete in a free market, so vendors love it when they can establish monopolies or something close to them; where there is little or no competition; where they are more or less free to set prices; and where they can dictate product content without too much worry that a competitor will underprice or overdeliver against them. Unfortunately, it falls to customers, who at least in theory determine who serves in government to guard against monopoly formation but over the years government has had a spotty record in that regard.

Natural monopolies form in big, infrastructure-intense lines of business, such as regional electric or gas industries. Most states regulate monopolies when that happens, ensuring they don't take unfair advantage of customers but still guaranteeing companies an adequate return on their huge investments for providing quality service. Electricity providers are an example of a regulated monopoly for which the regulation happens at the state level.

The Federal Communications Commission (FCC) does a good job regulating telephone systems and broadcast radio and TV, but so far has laid an egg with cable by releasing it from some of the same requirements9 that other infrastructure monopolies have to deal with. For instance, most other infrastructure monopolies are required to operate as common carriers, taking on all comers and delivering their services evenly and at reasonable prices. To date, Comcast and cable in general have avoided this burden, leading to contentiousness exemplified by the Comcast class-action suit.

All vendor-customer relationships tend toward the monopolistic. Whether or not there is competition during the initial purchase, once a customer commits to a vendor that vendor becomes the de facto monopolist in the account. If you drive Honda and not Ford, Honda's ecosystem becomes your default parts supplier. If you use the Oracle database you don't get updates from IBM. These specificities help create what many in the business world call walled gardens.

A walled garden is the next best thing to a monopoly because it effectively locks out competition (like a monopoly), while it acknowledges the customer's ability to choose — at least once as in the examples above. Often the walls of the garden have little to do with the vendor or product but a lot to do with ancillary issues, such as frequent-flier miles or any other investment that's sunk into acquiring and using a vendor's product line that can't easily be written off.

Customers very often feel trapped by their investments once a deal is done, and they sometimes don't feel like they have a voice in steering vendors' policies and decisions that affect them. But the business climate is changing and offering new models that offer more freedom for the customer at the cost of greater revenue risk for vendors.

The modern subscription model is the increasingly dominant business model in many industries today. The model is growing rapidly and is drawing customers because they have more freedom to move on whenever they wish, without regard to contracts or sunk costs. It's the model that's training the behavior of a new generation of customers and one that doesn't need the Supreme Court to keep customers in the fold. More on subscriptions in Chapter 3, but for now, let's look at how conventional vendors try to understand their customers to keep them coming back.

Net Promoter Score

You might think — wait a minute, there are lots of vendors in my business and personal life that I just don't care that much about. They deliver a product or service that's good enough and you don't give them another thought.

You know what? In their world, *you don't exist*. The reason why follows.

One of the most popular ways vendors measure how they're doing with customers is through the Net Promoter Score℠ (NPS®). As is true of all good metrics, it's a simple measurement based on readily available or collectible data and a simple calculation. Business strategist Fred F. Reichheld introduced the NPS in a 2003 *Harvard Business Review* article, "One Number You Need to Grow"[10] and later expanded in the book *The Ultimate Question: Driving Good Profits and True Growth*. Although there's some controversy about the NPS's predictive ability, it does offer some valid insight into a customer's sentiment about a vendor. When taken in aggregate it can give a sound assessment of how a group of customers view a vendor — an assessment that indirectly describes that company's ability to prosper.

The NPS runs along a continuum from -100 (everyone is a detractor) to +100 (everyone is a promoter); negative scores are bad and positive numbers are good. The score is based on a single question: "On a scale of zero to 10, how likely are you to refer to a friend or a colleague?" Table 1.1 describes scoring.

Score	Classification
0 – 6	Detractors
7 – 8	Passives
9 – 10	Promoters

Table 1.1 NPS scoring

The NPS is calculated by throwing out the passives and using the following equation:

% Promoters - % Detractors = NPS

So, let's say you have 100 responses to an NPS survey. If there are 10 people who rate your company as 0 to 6 on the scale and there are 20 who give you a 7 or 8, and 70 who give your company a 9 or 10, then the NPS works out to 70 – 10 = 60. Congratulations, you have an NPS of 60, which is quite good. You can now begin strategizing about what it would take to move some of those 20 passives into the promoter column to make your score even higher.

If you are one of those customers who never bother reviewing their vendor relationships — maybe you'd give them a 7 or an 8 in an NPS survey if you decided to bother with answering it at all — you don't count. Why? The answer is, companies don't mind getting scores in the middle. Those scores represent reasonably happy customers — certainly not the ones who would join a class-action suit — and they cancel out. Every company has a few sterling examples of customers who just dig what they do and would give them 9s or 10s, and as long as the 9s and 10s exceed the responses in the 0–6 range, vendors are reasonably happy. And nothing much changes.

Role of the business model

From the outside looking in, United's business model was at least part of the reason for the standoff and Comcast's model drove (and still drives) its aggressive territory-acquisition strategy. At the time of the United Breaks Guitars incident, United's business model was transaction oriented, as the business models of many older companies are. This transaction model might say, "You pay us money and we will take you to your destination. Anything else is not part of the plan, and we don't admit that there could be outcomes different from the few that we have programmed into our business (and our computers)."

In a transaction model the provider's responsibility ends when the product is delivered — in United's case, your arrival at your destination. This model makes money through large numbers of transactions with new or repeat customers. A company's growth depends on making more transactions, raising prices, and delivering new products to market, through which additional transactions can take place. There's little profit in any single transaction because today's vendors generally prefer large markets and large transaction volumes to fewer high-value transactions. That's what drives our modern consumer society, but it also helps explain why vendors can ignore individual complaints. No single customer or incident can derail a vendor for long.

The cable industry (or any subscription company) provides a service that is easily repeatable, but a region's population limits its customer base and revenues dribble in monthly. Subscription companies live for repeatable business, so having the ability to resell the same customers — especially if additional services are involved — is critical to a subscription company's good health, as is the ability to freeze out competition (e.g., in the case of clustering).

United's business model has been hamstrung by its industry's capacity glut — there are too many flights by too many carriers to the same destinations. That means a carrier can't raise prices without the risk of being undercut by a competitor, losing money and market share. It's also very hard to develop new routes to new destinations because the route structure is built out. If global warming opens up the beaches on the Aleutian Islands to summer tourism, the airlines would have new places to go, but absent something like that, it is what it is. With airlines continuing to merge in the past few years, carriers are now able to reduce duplication on some routes. The results are that prices are increasing on those routes and the industry itself is becoming more monopolistic.

It's also doubtful that airlines can add more customers to drive growth. Optimization software already has helped increase seat-occupancy rates[11] industry-wide, and many airlines have squeezed more seats into their plane cabins. Business travel declined during the recession and the Internet is replacing face-to-face meetings with virtual ones in the form of conferencing services like WebEx and ON24. Virtual meetings don't provide the experience of face-to-face meetings, but they're good enough, especially considering the time saved and the cost differential. In addition, people only have so much leisure time, the wealthy and middle-class populations are growing slowly, and the recession has put a crimp in how the middle class spends — all of which restricts the number of net new customers an airline can attract.

So, it's a zero-sum situation for many companies today. If customers choose your competition you lose out on that transaction. That's why frequent-flier programs are so important. People give a preferred carrier as much of their business as possible to concentrate the miles earned, sometimes even paying a slight premium over competing fares to fly that airline.

Cable providers like Comcast aren't very different. The cable industry's early days were spent hunting for new customers, but with increasing market saturation cable providers have had to begin farming the ones they have. That's why upselling — "Try our movie package or our phone service!" — and rate increases are so important. They're a significant source of company growth. It's also why customer retention is so vital today and why, if a company like United or Comcast is going to alienate its customers, that company had better have either a strong loyalty program with great perks or a defacto monopoly.

Making money

Despite the state of some public opinion, there are very few truly bad companies out there. Most businesses don't have the time or resources to do anything but stick to their business models, and many refer to those models as their secret sauce: *This is the way we make money, the secret of our success, don't even think about changing the recipe.* For most companies, the business models are so fundamental that they'd rather self-immolate than change them. One of the perennial challenges to installing a new technology system in any large company, for instance, is that the software must support the company's business model in total, even the parts that the software vendor is absolutely sure don't make any sense. As a result, software systems have become the conscience-free enforcers of many companies' business models at the very moment when customers want more than the models might provide. And customers have gained new ways to advertise any displeasure with those models.

People, Process, and Technology

If there are very few bad companies out there and if company employees are not a bunch of "bad apples," then how did we get to the position where customers are too eager to sue vendors or bad-mouth them? Perhaps there's something else going on, something we've overlooked in the constant effort to analyze business and boil it down to profit and loss. There are more dimensions to business than that because fickle, imprecise, emotional humans conduct business. But what's missing in many business situations, ironically, is any sense of humanity. It's a paradox that customers and employees are all people and yet the two groups sometimes treat each other as if they were parts of different species.

The roots of the problem and the solution can be found in the old business standbys: people, process, and technology (PPT). They got us into the current situation and they will be helpful in getting us out. The existing PPTs, however, were trained and designed to support a business paradigm that is rapidly disappearing; they need to be replaced by a new generation of PPT that are right for the times.

Altruism and empathy — In *business*? Yup.

Vendors have set up their businesses to deal with transactions — lots of them. But while vendors may operate with a transaction mindset, customers don't. They engage in transactions, of course, but only at the end of a *process*. They may buy things, but only after kicking the proverbial tires, trying them on, giving them a workout — whatever they do, it can take time. Simply put, vendors prepare for transactions, but customers expect processes.

This friction goes a long way toward explaining many things. Incredibly, we all keep both of these ideas in our heads at once. We may work as vendors in support of transactions, but as customers we want and need processes that educate us, enable us to make decisions, and get service. This is one of the great business conundrums of our time and one that's enshrined in our computer systems.

Companies have built elaborate, computerized customer interfaces over the past 30 years to drive efficiency into business processes that were thought to be inefficient due to human involvement. In place of human contact and the ability to reason that goes with it, we have algorithms that capture essential customer data, process it, and arrive at scores that dictate the next steps in customer transactions. A credit rating is one prominent example. In financial transactions, a person's credit score is a critical determinant of whether credit is extended for a purchase, and is therefore the gateway for many transactions.

But why do customers devote such energy to behaving like the Comcast litigants or Dave Carroll? It's not simple frustration or anger. There are other emotional components at work: Some people who raise a stink are like jilted lovers; some may be acting to help warn others.

The answer might involve altruism, a characteristic emotion that humans share with a small number of other highly intelligent animals. Altruism involves unselfish behavior that a person might engage in to help the group even though that behavior might be dangerous to the individual. The usual example of altruism involves an animal giving a warning cry to alert others about the presence of a predator. People exhibit altruism all the time.

Was Dave Carroll being altruistic? Certainly, he behaved in a way that was to his disadvantage when you consider the time and effort he put into his crusade. Much the same can be said about the Comcast litigants, although the law firm representing them made most of the effort. There are enough examples in the business world today — the Comcast class action and Dave Carroll are far from unique.

And what about empathy? Empathizing is putting yourself into someone else's shoes; it's another trait shared by intelligent animals, especially mammals. Empathy should be the primary motivator of customer relationships. When a company loses empathy for its customers it begins to treat them as mere consumers — a slippery slope with no good outcome.

People who joined the Comcast class action and those who viewed, endorsed, and shared Dave Carroll's videos, were perhaps following an altruistic impulse to warn others about interactions where vendor empathy did not exist. We dress the idea up in business terms and call it word of mouth, but it's just plain being human.

For a long time, word of mouth was exactly that: the verbal communication to one person (or a small group) at a time. Word of mouth can be extremely powerful. It has been responsible for building up and tearing down political candidates, making hit records and movies, and establishing the popularity of almost any product. Word of mouth is an inherently social phenomenon; today, with social media to amplify it, word of mouth has become a potent force in business. Many companies have already adopted social media as new communication tools for advertising, but social's biggest use and greatest benefit is not the ability to broadcast offers to customers. Social's greatest power is in its unique capability to enable vendors to listen to huge groups of customers long before they get mad. Social listening demonstrates a business' empathy for its customers.

But for all the progress that's been made in adopting modern communication channels and techniques, there are many companies that have yet to embrace change. They're the late adopters and to a degree, you can tell who they are by the ferocity of their customers.

We've gradually gotten away from empathy in the key relationships between vendors and customers over the past few decades, and customer altruism has made some bizarre accommodations to that reality. Computer systems that were little more than electronic filing cabinets or systems of record began to replace the human element, first by making record-keeping more efficient and later by replacing human decision making with scoring and weighting algorithms, and sometimes-too-rigid business rules. At other times, such as the great banking meltdown of 2008, the rules were too loose. How do we get to rules that are just right? Maybe we need a new way to think about rules.

At the same time, communications options have exploded. Thanks to shifts ranging from the deregulation of the telephone industry to the vast, fast, and free capabilities of social media and the Internet, altruistic human tendencies have been able to expand beyond the small towns of only a generation ago to a global market. Today's customers are acutely attuned to vendor misdeeds, whether domestic or foreign or by commission or omission, and they can act on any perceived slight much faster than many of the corporations whose computer systems, social and otherwise, have not kept up. Too often an apparent misdeed starts as an innocuous attempt to improve business results and metastasizes to something more destructive when a vendor overlooks or fails to see a mistake until it's too late.

In the balancing act between customer and vendor, altruism and empathy must be harnessed to produce relationships that are good for both parties. But empathy for the customer must come first. It's the way of courtship, after all. Some researchers will call this the beginnings of a conversation about *the customer experience* — but the meaning of that phrase has quickly narrowed to a description of the moment of purchase, a transaction. This is more.

SftC Takeaways

1. All vendor (mis)deeds can be easily scrutinized today, placing new emphasis on doing the right thing.

2. Lack of vendor empathy can raise customer altruism in ways you may not like.

3. People, process, and technology must balance.

The following chapters demonstrate that the true customer experience should be so much more than a transaction. But changing the customer's experience with any aspect of a company is far from easy because experience is tightly intertwined with many companies' business models.

Chapter Two

Old Business Models Contribute to the Problem

What's changed? Customers went off in one direction while business models stayed more or less the same. It's time the two reunited.

For the past century, according to economic and social theorist Jeremy Rifkin, business has operated on the assumption that vertically integrated companies "...create economies of scale and highly rationalized corporate bureaucracies — with centralized management and top-down command-and-control mechanisms — to organize commercial life."[1]

Customers were placed at the bottom of the hierarchy and called consumers because in this schema it was their job to consume whatever the corporations produced. I like capitalism — warts and all — but Rifkin proposes that it's at least due for a makeover. My research suggests that customers are driving the change.

In industry after industry, such as publishing, music, and entertainment, the marginal cost of selling one more widget is (or has fallen to) almost zero, zip, nada, making the product virtually free. Not to put too fine a point on it, but Rifkin also says, "If that were to happen, profit, the lifeblood of capitalism, would dry up."[2]

Actually, in many of the markets most exposed to the Internet, such as the music industry, that's already happening. The cost of producing (or stealing) one more CD is just about zero and the music companies and bands are feeling it. Their newer survival strategies all center on having good relationships with fans so that they can sell other things like performances and merchandise. In a zero marginal-cost society, the thing you sell is time and expertise, not a product. Products are table stakes.

Customers are driving changes in your business model and the arrangement of PPTs that got us through a vertically integrated, command-and-control 20th century are a poor fit for what's coming. To say that business models are changing also implies that the PPTs we've grown to depend on are up for a rethink, too.

Business Model

United and Comcast offer great examples of the vertically integrated business model. You might be surprised to see Comcast lumped in with United; after all, it's a subscription service and subscriptions are the new, new thing — right? They're the business model of the future. Comcast sells subscriptions but acts more like a monopoly than like a true subscription service. Like Comcast, subscription companies have annual contracts and charge monthly fees but you can drop a subscription at the end of the contract or, if you don't have a contract, you can drop out after the billing period has expired. Most important, in a subscription market there are often other vendors that can serve your needs. In cable you can sign up with another vendor, if one exists in your area.

But in many areas there is only one supplier because the huge cost of building a cable infrastructure prohibits another vendor from coming into the market. Verizon and ATT are telephone companies regulated somewhat differently from Comcast, according to Crawford[3], and even they find it challenging to compete in cable against the likes of Comcast. In the Philadelphia Comcast suit, the class action revolved around Comcast's acquisition of a competitor, which significantly reduced competition and let Comcast behave as it wanted.

Subscriptions only

Against the conventional 20th century business model (and even today's), an emerging model — subscriptions — is changing the landscape and teaching customers to expect more from their vendors. Vendors in all industries have been slow to adopt subscriptions because lower fees reduce revenue flows and distort their companies' value to Wall Street. But customers want what they want and subscriptions increasingly are seen as the way to satisfy them.

The modern subscription model is based on the idea that customers can and do abandon their suppliers and that vendors are in constant recruitment and customer-accommodation mode. For customers in a zero marginal–cost society, it's much less important to own something than it is to have access to its more-or-less exclusive use. The subscription model started in many places at once and early successes came in enterprise software by vendors like Salesforce.com and NetSuite. But you can go back farther to cellular services and car leases to see the origins of what is now called the subscription economy.

Subscriptions have some common features that make them very attractive to customers: They are time-bound (you sign up to use a service for a period of time) and you pay a small fee for that use, much smaller than you'd spend for a purchase, and there's no need to monitor your subscription unless you want to renew it (vendors usually take responsibility for getting the renewal). There's no possibility that you'll continue paying for something you no longer want unless you sign up for automatic renewal and don't pay attention.

Say you lease a car for three years. During that time you treat it as your own, with some minor exceptions (you can't sell a leased vehicle). It's the same with cellular services, which are bound in some respects. For instance, your agreement provides a specified number of minutes for various features (voice, messaging, and Internet access). If you use more than your contracted allotment, you pay a previously agreed-to fee that's in your contract.

The subscription economy has provided an extra boost to many businesses' market penetration efforts by making their products more affordable, thus expanding the size of addressable markets. Most important, subscription vendors have changed how business is pursued. Their business systems collect huge amounts of data about customers, such as their usage habits and their payment histories. Savvy subscription vendors analyze all this data for inflection points, seasonal variation, opportunities to cross- or upsell, and early customer-dissatisfaction warning signs, which may lead to churn or attrition. So customer dissatisfaction is to be avoided at all costs to prevent bad outcomes that reduce revenue and require additional sales and marketing efforts to overcome. Enhanced data collection and analysis is one of the driving forces behind subscriptions' success because it enables vendors to better understand customers.

More on subscriptions in Chapter 3, but for now, let's say that the use of subscriptions has changed how customers regard vendors and how some vendors behave in the marketplace.

Subscribers

As subscribers, customers increasingly expect very low prices, high levels of product functionality and intuitiveness, and closer relationships with vendors. The social revolution has made us all expect instant responses for a wide range of comments and inquiry, and if a response is not forthcoming we think something is wrong. We also expect that as long as there's a glimmer of a Wi-Fi–service bar on our mobile devices we can connect with our vendors and that they'll know our histories, our purchases, and have a good idea of what we need.

This all adds up to higher customer expectations of experiences with a brand, a product, or a vendor. We now have a subscription economy, and we are becoming a subscription culture. The reality that vendors must grapple with is that customers expect subscription-grade experiences whenever they deal with vendors, regardless of whether those vendors operate a conventional business or issue subscriptions.

Technology

Surprisingly, technology's diffusion into the subscription culture is lagging. My mother-in-law is a skilled iPhone user (and she is just as good with her iPad and iMac), but while she may be exceptional now, her peers also are quickly moving down the adoption curve. But end-user technology is only part of the picture — often the easy part. As customers, she and millions of others have the tools to engage at very high levels with vendors that don't always reciprocate. On the vendor side, once bought, customer-facing technology can remain in place for many years, changed only by an upgrade cycle. Importantly, the business processes this technology is supposed to manage are frozen in time.

An obvious part of the technology vector is software. Part of the issue between vendors and customers today is the reality that systems of record that might have been installed at the turn of the century have been modified to become customer-facing systems today. Companies put a friendly enough browser interface in front of records data, perhaps add a few dozen algorithms to help customers navigate, and then christen these new apps as self-service systems.

But those systems were intended to assist employees to retrieve information in what were manual customer-facing processes; they were not intended to serve end users who have an imperfect understanding of a company and its policies. There is a mismatch between these systems of record and the processes that customers expect are managed by systems of engagement.

Net/Net

Vendors have set up their businesses to deal with transactions — lots of them. But while they operate with a transaction mindset, customers no longer do. They've emerged into a great common space where they expect to interact with vendors in many channels, through many devices, and at any time, and they expect to engage in relevant processes that may or may not result in what a vendor would recognize as a transaction. Sadly, many vendors still don't understand what's happening to their markets. They may not even be aware of the deep reserves of anger and distrust that their aging systems produce.

Customer Sentiment Matters

There's an Internet meme about how the Internet makes it possible for customers to influence many more people than they ever could when the telephone was their only communication device. In the past, this meme goes, people could tell their closest friends and acquaintances about a bad vendor experience but the reporting of that experience was limited because individuals didn't have a mass-marketing utility for broadcasting their opinions. This ability to broadcast any content — in some cases indiscriminately — that may or may not be true may have the farthest-reaching consequences for vendors. It has complicated life for many, if not most of them.

As we saw in United Breaks Guitars, after spending decades and many millions of dollars building a brand, a company's reputation can take a serious hit if just a few people state their case (regardless of its merits) on the Internet. This situation can make a marketer long for the days of class-action lawsuits and tight-lipped litigants.

In the age of customer sentiment people can and do share how they feel about vendors and products with perfect strangers. One interpretation is that these people are acting altruistically by alerting others to a problem, and perhaps many are. But it can be hard to determine fact from opinion on the Internet, and some people don't even try.

That's the nub of the problem — opinions are *not* facts. Sentiment conveys opinion, but sentiment may not be factual; in an age of free expression, few people bother to confirm the judgments of others. Consequently, vendors need to engineer customer interactions as if they were products — many of them are in the sense of whole product (see the Introduction). A whole product is everything from the core product itself to training, support, service, policies and procedures, and more. Some people call this the customer experience, but I think *whole product* is more concrete than that.

Whole Product

Early-stage companies or even mature companies entering early-stage markets often have less defined whole products. These companies focus on delivering an innovative offering to early-adopter customers who don't expect much beyond the merchandise itself. But as markets mature, customers expect well-articulated solutions. This can come as a shock to an emerging company trying to play in a rapidly expanding market. The need for well-articulated whole product can put a brake on any company's growth, but this is especially true of an emerging company.

Too often a company's knee-jerk response to this need is automation, but unless it's well planned, an automation strategy can hamper customer success rather than enable it. For instance, in customer relationship management (CRM), call center automation was at first a boon to customer service, but these systems quickly became swamped by the volume of customer demand. Many companies could not afford the seemingly infinite expansion the demand required. Faced with waiting on hold or finding their own answers, many customers chose the latter solution. The result? Rather than helping customers, these systems only served to deflect them. Those deflections weaken customer bonds and represent a vendor failure in a moment of truth.

Plan B

The surge of sentiment in the Internet Age is the result of numerous attempts by regular people to take on corporations in lone-wolf efforts to punish these companies for transgressions (both real and imagined). Say what you will of United Breaks Guitars, but it looks a lot like one such attempt, regardless of its merits, and it has likely spawned imitators.

Historically, vendors have chosen not to engage with the naysayers; it would only call attention to their cause. This might have been a good policy before the Internet's version of everyman's bully pulpit. But now, people research vendors through search engines, communities, and other freely available Internet services and there's more at stake. If this were about high-quality manufacturing, the solution would involve eliminating as many risk factors for defects as possible — not a bad idea for dealing with customers today. In the front office this involves understanding sentiment and taking customer-centric approaches to head off the worst effects before they gain steam.

The mass-market approach to customers often designs sentiment out of the picture by reducing the customer to a consumer. For many companies and for a long time, customer sentiment was an unknown quantity for two reasons: There were few reliable, effective, and inexpensive ways to capture it, and there were few business processes that actually used this valuable information.

Taking customer sentiment into consideration is a new way of doing business that many organizations are working hard to understand and adopt. Their adoption failure or tardiness helps explain why customers form class actions and create videos and songs about their experiences. All of this gives the customer a kind of validation that many vendors are ill equipped to provide on their own at the moment. But these customer actions, while enlightening, are only some of the more extreme examples of customers demanding to be acknowledged by their vendors, they are the canary in a very big coalmine. Even more creative, though arguably less effective approaches litter the Internet as this chapter illustrates.

As we've seen, customer sentiment means how customers feel and their opinions — what they're willing to say about your company or brand to their peers. Given that definition, it's amazing that more vendors don't yet express deep understanding of their customers' sentiments (though some leaders do take customer sentiment seriously).

Plan B involves overtly collecting customer data, including data about opinions, use characteristics, unmet needs, and more. It also involves analyzing that data to discover what customers think generally. To this point, sentiment can be used to help deal with individual customer issues and to drive more quantitative study. For instance, a qualitative sentiment analysis might reveal that people are tired of basic black as the only color for their Model T Fords. But what only quantitative research can then tell is that 37 percent prefers red, 19 percent wants white, 39 percent likes blue, and the remaining 5 percent doesn't care. It all works together.

Analyzing customer sentiment — What sucks?

Customer sentiment and its analysis start with the customer-loyalty metric, NPS (see Chapter 1). The NPS tells you how customers felt at one point in time, and whether at that moment they would recommend a vendor if asked. But of necessity, NPS looks back; it doesn't predict the future to a great degree. For example, it only asks if a customer would recommend, not if a customer already had recommended. There's a big difference.

Today, customer sentiment is online, always available, and constantly changing. Think of it as a stock ticker that's updated as frequently as you want, depending on the technology you use. Customers express sentiment in many ways and places. Using social media like Twitter they can describe a recent experience even while they are in the moment. For example, this tweet

@DenisPombriant #SFTC rocks!

is directed at this author and the meaning of the message is clear — if self-serving.

Twitter enables other users to retweet on to their followers and in a short time, if the content is judged to be important enough, many thousands of people can receive the message and resend it to their followers, too. It's the reason that vendors need ways to know what people are saying about them (i.e., customer sentiment).

Figuring out what customers are saying is getting easier. Sentiment-analysis software searches social streams looking for keywords and symbols. A user of sentiment analytics might deploy such a system to check for all mentions of his or her Twitter handle like @DenisPombriant or all mentions of something like a book, a conference, a product (#SFTC). The resulting filtered stream can provide powerful real-time insight into what's happening in the marketplace and give a vendor or other interested party the time and information to take action. For example, looking for multiple things like @companyname, #productname and #problem can do a lot to enable a vendor to be in the moment with a customer.

Last, sentiment analytics are really good at ferreting out important keywords like rocks, sucks, problem, help! — almost anything, and in multiple languages. Sentiment analytics are not limited to attitudinal analysis; they can also show intent to purchase, leadership or influence by one party over others, even emotions like anger. By using sentiment analysis, anyone who wants to can get a complete picture of our social media Zeitgeist and give an appropriate response.

It wasn't always like this. Before sentiment analysis (and today, to a great degree), customer sentiment was hidden in plain sight on the Internet. How? An earlier generation of customers who became frustrated with vendors for any reason could take it upon themselves to create web presences — websites, blogs, communities and the like — dedicated to exposing the alleged shortcomings of vendors or any product or entity (think about our altruism discussion in Chapter 1). Social media is like an anabolic steroid, amplifying actions and emotions like altruism. Sometimes, the results are not very empathetic.

These web properties all seem to have one thing in common and anyone can create one. Simply pick a name of an entity like ABCompany and add the word *sucks* to it and bingo, you've got a unique term, and unless someone else has already done so, you can apply for the domain name, get a URL, and build a site on which you can torture your transgressor.

Don't sue me, I am just reporting this

So what sucks? Just go to your favorite search engine and type in the name of any vendor or product, add sucks, stand back, and be prepared to have your hair curl.

All this dubious sentiment is bottled up in search engine protocol. You usually don't find *ABCompany sucks* when you do a search on the company so you may not even know these sites exist. Customers who may have had legitimate beefs with vendors have traded their right to be heard or to influence others for a moment of rage. Vendors are grateful that the search engine doesn't reveal these sites until you've scrolled down many, many pages.

When I was researching sentiment a few years ago (it was the new, new, new thing), I did a little experiment. I did my own sucks analysis and discovered that in almost any industry, you could stack rank the competitors by how much customers thought they sucked. And remember, this analysis only documents the people who were so mad that they invested significant time, effort, and even a little cash to pursue this misguided hobby. How many others just fumed?

Table 2.1 illustrates examples from my unscientific survey, which I repeated for *Solve for the Customer*. I call the numbers Sucks Scores, and they represent the number of hits the phrase's search returned, always in a fraction of a second. But beware: It's unscientific for several reasons. I used Google to search on "companyname sucks," but given the huge numbers returned it's impossible to verify that each and every listing is correctly tabulated. For all we know, somewhere in the millions of hits there may be some unclassifiable valentines to a vendor.

There are more sophisticated approaches that seem to back up my ad hoc survey, but for now, consider this a first approximation. Also, keep in mind that this kind of analysis works more reliably for American or Western companies.

Company	Sucks score
Exxon Mobil	5,500,000
Wal-Mart Stores	11,700,000
Royal Dutch Shell	1,490,000
BP	16,900,000
General Motors	651,000
Chevron	448,000
Toyota Motor	307,000
Ford Motor	738,000
ConocoPhillips	618,000

Table 2.1 Sucks Scores for Some Big Companies

We can get some impressive Sucks Scores for Chinese banks, but it's unclear if the results are of the same quality as what we find for

Western banks. Some of the results for foreign banks have real news interspersed with what sucks and while the word *sucks* might be translatable, it is not universal. In addition, when appraising a company in a country with a totalitarian government you just don't know — it might be a capital crime to slander a hard-working bank there. For all these reasons those results might not be very reliable. Last, results for companies engaged in multiple lines of business like telecommunications companies offering wired phone service, cable, and cable phone, and more might have different scores by line of business. You might want to search by brand or the line of business. It's not always easy to tease apart the sentiment in these cases.

Sentiment can be positive as well as negative — just like in the NPS formula (see Chapter 1) — even in markets where sentiment seems to run consistently against most vendors. Take fast food, for instance. With all we know about salt, fat, and carbohydrates in fast food you might expect that the industry's Sucks Scores would be high. But we like fast food, according to the Sucks Scores. In fact, I think most airlines would love to have the Sucks Scores of a middle-of-the-road fast-food merchant. Positive sentiment in such markets gives hope to all of us that changing business practices yields good results in sentiment analysis.

If you wanted a greater context you could create a metric or a formula that includes this raw data divided by the number of customers or net revenues or profits. But that would be creative accounting. Even one detractor customer is too many, so what use would it be to know the number of really angry customers per million dollars of revenue or profits? Is there a number that's acceptable? Acceptability is a slippery slope that we might have to accept at some point, but the goal should be zero defects.

In this kind of analysis I've seen oil companies get hit pretty hard (as have airlines and big banks). Any industry — from fast food to cars to telecommunications companies to cable providers — can be stack ranked this way. Even Ivy League universities can be stack ranked. In any big industry that materially affects your life so that you can't live with it and you can't live without it, the top vendors routinely get their hats handed to them in the raw data of a Sucks analysis. Today, there are somewhat more accurate approaches. Someday, the era of Suck Scores might be remembered as the good old days.

Customer Sentiment — The Zeitgeist

In the best tradition of for-profit business and the Internet, amateur efforts to convey displeasure have given rise to commercial endeavors that serve up negative sentiment along with a side of advertisements. Sites like Pissedconsumer.com, Ripoffreport.com, Complaintsboard.com, Consumerist.com, and My3cents.com will tell you customer sentiment as they collect it (which may not win any prizes for scientific method). Sadly, the venerable Consumerunion.org gets lumped into this group, too, but Consumers' Union is a trusted customer data collector and does good analysis.

These sites document what appear to be true testimonials, complete with misspellings, of people's frustrations with vendors and often the frustrations seem genuine. Following are some examples. (References to particular companies have been removed, giving them the benefit of the doubt.)

Pissed consumer.com

On Pissedconsumer.com you can submit a complaint, browse other complaints, hit the blog, or get a filtered listing of complaints about industries and vendors by keyword. Since anyone can submit a claim or report, not all of them are well written or researched, and some give distinct impression that the author has not kept up with current events: "Amazon.com search, filting (sic) and sorting results appear to be rigged."

"xxx Bank stole my cahs (sic) rewards"

"xxx Bank — modification request not properly handled, home in foreclosure"

"xxx Bank — I was lied to"

Ripoffreport.com

Ripoffreport.com is a good site because it lets you file a detailed account of the transgression. And there are interesting additional buttons on each report, including, "Add Rebuttal to this Report," "Arbitrate and Set Record Straight," "File New Report," and "Repair your reputation." Here, some recent headlines:

"xxx Airlines Unscrupulous, xxx Airlines Steals Money!"

"xxx Airlines Ripoff. Abuse, incompetence Houston Texas"

"xxx Airlines ... not a good way to start or finish a vacation, Chicago, Illinois"

Complaintsboard.com

Complaintsboard.com wraps itself in democracy with its tagline, "Made by the people, for the people" while another tagline says "The most trusted and popular consumer complaints website" though it gives no authentication for these claims. As with other sites you can submit a complaint or a photo, and you can ask questions of a community (of sorts). There's also a "News & Stories" tab that appears to be republishing some vendor press releases.

The site looks like a message board where anyone can log an issue and others can comment on it. There doesn't appear to be any consolidation or analytics capability. Sample headlines under fast food include:

"xxx — Constant wrong orders!"

"xxx — Discrimination"

"xxx — Price discrepancy"

"xxx — Dirty hands of employees, Rude behavior"

Consumerist.com

Consumerist.com appears to be a blog, the writers have bylines, and it seems like a muckraking operation in the best sense of the word. The stories seem journalistic, not random rants. Visitors can "Submit a Tip" for the writers to cover and the site doesn't support ads. Instead, there's a big "Donate" button to attract subscribers.

The About Us tab states: "To send a tip to our editorial staff, write to tips@consumerist.com. Please understand that you are contacting journalists and all emails will be considered submissions for publication unless you explicitly request otherwise."

Sample headlines:

"Why Did My Free Gift Card Cost $10?"

"Target, Where Condoms Are a Suggested Substitute for Antacid."

This story is about Target's automated, suggested substitutions: "We are sold out of: 32 ct. Tums Ultra chewy, cherry antacids (245-05-0141). Please substitute: 10-ct. Trojan bare skin condoms (245-03-0387)." Clearly, Target has a sense of humor, and a little more programming to do.

The point is that vendors can no longer ignore customer complaints because in some cases vendors are causing real pain by doing nothing (or by appearing to). They're also self-inflicting injuries that ought to be avoided. Business models have to change and systems have to be rethought, rebuilt, and simplified to meet the growing online demands of this marketplace. But where to start?

Starting Point

Take a moment to reread the sentiments above. The thing that strikes me about these examples and the many, many more online is that most refer not to a transaction that went bad but to a process that did, and caused some harm to the customer. That's an important distinction that reinforces the fact that customers think in terms of process, while vendors think about transactions.

Bonding

Let's begin by examining the way we bond. There's no shortage of things to blame for the sometimes-smoldering state of relations between vendors and customers. If we're going to get anywhere we need to establish bonding (see Chapter 4) as the starting point that organizes the effort to tone down the anger.

Advances in technology and business models have loosened the bonds between vendors and customers. The business models in many industries have made direct customer contact less likely, having replaced personal interaction with machines and algorithms that don't always get the job done. In many cases this automation is good but not good enough. They support transactions at a time when customers feel the absence of processes. A true process will not allow the kinds of mishaps complained about in sentiment sites, because a true process will always gracefully loop back to a helpful, informed employee.

When I was a kid my parents had lots of choices about which vendors they would do business with in our community. Often you couldn't tell much difference between two hardware stores or two furniture stores but we'd give all our business to one. We were bonded not by some superficial device that locked us into the relationship but by choice. My dad knew the people at those places and they knew him, too. They went to school and maybe church together, suffered through some of the worst parts of the Great Depression, and had similar military experiences and might have shared similar job histories. They were bonded in ways that contracts and frequent flier miles couldn't touch. We have a different society today and share fewer experiences, in addition to that lack of personal contact. The technology that's all around us can shorten the distances between vendors and customers — if we apply it.

SftC Takeaways

1. Business models that assume customers are mere consumers can lead to inadequate customer outreach.

2. You get the systems and technologies that your business models dictate and if either is more than 10 years old, it's becoming a drag on your business.

3. Regardless of your model, your customers are becoming subscribers and their mindset is to seek alternative suppliers if you disappoint them.

4. Customer sentiment is easily spread so you need to ensure that it's positive.

Chapter 3 explains why the subscription business model has become so important in numerous markets.

Chapter Three

The Power of the Subscription Model

Customers gain the upper hand when markets commoditize, as they have over the past few years. Subscriptions are one of the commoditization vehicles in place today; they are returning to customers some of the autonomy they lost at the start of the information revolution several decades ago.

Subscriptions also are changing the marketplace (altering how customers buy), and in the process they're changing vendors. The Internet and social media revolutions have changed people, too, enabling them to be more effective communicators and more assertive in their dealings in the marketplace. But there is one more change agent to consider, a curveball, affecting how customers relate to vendors today. Ironically, it's something that the vendor community started that now produces some blowback for them.

The blowback is that although this business model makes it super-easy to attract new customers, they can walk away without notice. There are very few tethers in subscriptions holding customers in vendors' orbits other than great relationships built on trust and service that concretely demonstrate vendor empathy. Sometimes, that builds fierce loyalty. There is also some irony that the Internet and devices like social media and sentiment sites give customers a voice while subscriptions give them mobility. Vendors inadvertently taught customers to be independent through the subscription business model — it's no surprise that customers have taken to it like a cat to an unmade bed.

Subscriptions aren't the end of the new business-model story. We're now witnessing the burgeoning of many other business models, such as the sharing model[1], based on old-fashioned barter. Sharing goes farther than subscriptions by reducing the cost of use to almost zero in many cases favoring collaborative ownership or sequential consumption. For instance, imagine a neighborhood lawnmower rather than every family owning one. Some of these models might turn out to be fads but they are changing the way that vendors and customers engage, which is another reason to view purchasers as customers and not consumers (see Chapter 2).

But know this — as customer-oriented business models proliferate they are changing the conventional vendor-customer relationship in fundamental ways. Relationships have moved online and they're becoming asynchronous, enabling customers to check in at their convenience, forcing vendors to accept the need for capturing customer data that they then piece together into the information that drives their commercial success. Most interestingly, even conventional business models are coming in for haircuts.

The Subscription Economy

You could see it coming. There is an abundant supply of things to buy but demand has been throttled back by a long recession and stagnant income growth. Also, in many economies the emerging middle class can't afford to purchase all its needs, so subscriptions fill a vital need for many necessities of middle-class life. People and businesses need many things but they have limited capacities for buying everything. The market-oriented solution was the evolution of subscriptions, a way to deliver products as if they were services. In practice that means making greatly reduced periodic payments with no expectation of transferring ownership. You could think of it as a form of perpetual vendor financing. It keeps vendors and customers engaged in mutually beneficial relationships and it places a new set of imperatives on vendors to stay abreast of customers' wants, needs, and sentiments (or risk losing them).

Subscriptions have already changed the marketplace. Renting a car is subscribing to transportation services — so is leasing one for three years or using a ZipCar by the hour. The major difference is the duration of use. ZipCar's "Wheels when you want them" motto neatly summarizes the company's business model, which includes positioning rental cars around cities where ZipCar club members can take them for as little as an hour at a time all for a fixed price and with no strings attached — gas and insurance are included in the rental price.

Cell phone plans are subscriptions, although the subscriber keeps the device (even though the two-year subscription term is about equal to two generations of phones and at the end of the subscription it's likely the subscriber will replace the device).

The many wine-of-the-month clubs? You receive bottles of wine but the clubs are really services in which vendors carefully select, package, and ship wines based your previously submitted preferences. Does this make them wine advisory-and-delivery services? Probably.

It's more or less the same with razors from The Dollar Shave Club, and a variety of clothing (Rent the Runway), housewares (Lost Crates), grooming supplies (Birchbox Man or Birchbox Woman), and almost anything else you can think of (The Dollar Rubber Club really exists.). Subscriptions are so successful that we forget that we're subscribing to a service. What's a diet or a dating site if not a subscription to one of those specialized services?

More than financial benefits

Subscribers can save a bundle by accessing products as services rather than making a product purchase — if a purchase is even possible, but in many cases the added benefit is convenience. ZipCar users, for example, use other forms of transportation like a subway or taxi much of the time, but get a car for specific reasons like going on a date or taking a large vehicle to bring big items home from a store. In part, ZipCar users get value by eliminating the hassles of car ownership (the expense of buying and financing a car, fueling, insuring, and maintaining it, as well as parking — especially in a city — and paying excise taxes. All of those costs are rolled into the hourly cost of the rental. When the rental is over, so are the charges.

Subscriptions are not just for the B2C trade, either. The business-software industry started subscription services; B2B companies like Salesforce.com, NetSuite, and now thousands of others, deliver robust business software as a service (SaaS).

Many of the largest corporations in the world now use subscription business systems because they are cost effective, the vendors are very responsive, and the software is continuously updated to fix issues and, more often, to add functionality. The software also runs within moments of plunking down a credit card — something you can't usually expect from buying a software license.

There are many other types of software that are built to support novel business processes made possible by the social and mobile revolution. You can subscribe to them, too, frequently through one of the online-application storefronts these vendors maintain for their ecosystem partners.

So, no matter where you look customers are learning to be subscribers and they like it. An important point: Customers are applying their new understanding of the subscription paradigm to their expectations of non-subscription vendors. In the process they are taking greater latitude in how they deal with their vendors, which might rightly concern old-school vendors unaccustomed to this new approach to business.

The fact is that we have built not just a subscription economy, but also a subscription culture, one that (combined with other factors) has at once liberated customers and made us more demanding.

Customer and vendor latitude

Subscriptions are a very different way of doing business though they may not appear that different because their deliverables are so familiar. For customers, subscriptions provide great latitude not only in what they subscribe to but also to the terms of service.

For example, a subscription customer can purchase no-contract services with a recurring use-and-payment period (say, monthly). The customer can use the service from month-to-month and simply quit whenever it's convenient. Some vendors offer contracts that lock in prices and deliverables for periods ranging from one to three years. At the end of that time, unless the relationship is renewed, it's over — there's no further use of the service and the customer is completely free to go to another vendor.

In addition, in most cases a customer can elect to alter most aspects of the subscription at any time, increasing or decreasing or suspending service for a time. The configuration of the subscription is limited only by what the vendor packages and sells and what the customer decides to buy.

Vendors have great latitude with subscriptions to invent line-item products in unique combinations designed to suit the perceived demand very quickly. Unlike a conventional business model, where products have to be meticulously researched and field tested, subscription vendors have to do little more than make the world aware of a new offering. If it succeeds, great! If it fails, the cost of failure is tiny.

The real risk for a vendor is what happens if the customers stop coming or quit renewing. How do you forecast that? How do you forecast anything? More on this below, but whether or not you are a subscription business, chances are good (and getting better) that your customers think like subscribers — so, caveat venditor.

Vendor Beware

When was the last time you heard *vendor* beware? For subscription vendors (and, increasingly, everyone in the market), there is absolutely no substitute for keeping customers satisfied *and* delighted, because they can and do vote with their feet.

Subscriptions have been popularized by millennials — many of whom struggle with college debt and have poor job prospects — because the model allows them to have the goods and services they need, but can't afford, to purchase outright. It's spreading through other demographic groups like gen x-ers and boomers. It helps that these generations are also people who live on the Internet, an ideal medium for subscription companies to promote themselves for almost no cost. It's the same place where, through their computers, tablets, and handheld devices, people can and do trade experiences about vendors with their friends.

All of this is happening at an accelerating pace and vendors are finding that they need to adjust their product lines, pricing, and delivery options, as well as how they provide service and how they pay attention to customer needs. The good news for vendors is that a typical subscriber emits vastly more data about needs, preferences, and use than a conventional customer who makes a one-time purchase. The bad news is that if vendors haven't already made an attempt to capture conventional customer data, they have a lot of catching up to do as they and their customers turn to a subscription mindset.

Managing Companies in a Subscription Culture

Subscriptions provide some insight into how companies need to evolve to manage their customer interactions. The subscription vendor can learn and understand a great deal about its subscribers simply by capturing and analyzing usage and financial data. It's a good start, but it only addresses revenue and uptake — not issues of satisfaction with business processes and company practices (other than to give customers a way out of a bad relationship). Understanding customers as subscribers with the freedom to come and go as they please is important, but there's more to consider.

Savvy subscription company managers are always trying to know more about three things: customer attrition, recurring revenue, and the cost of acquiring revenue. You might think these are obvious or you might think they're not the most important issues that a subscription company has to deal with. Perhaps your thoughts are oriented toward the supply chain. That's important, too, but if you have a subscription business you won't have any information to inform your supply chain with if you don't also keep an eye on these three basic subscription drivers. In a research interview for *Solve for the Customer,* Tien Tzuo, CEO and cofounder of Zuora, a subscription-billing service designed for the needs of subscription vendors, says, "You can only derive recurring revenues from customers who are happily using your service. This sentiment directly translates into retention rates and churn reduction, both of which impact the revenue growth and financial health of any subscription business." So let's look at what this means.

Attrition

Customers come and go in a subscription business model. The trick is to hang on to them as long as possible because that old saying that it's less expensive to sell to an existing customer than it is to recruit a new one is true in spades for subscription vendors. It's fairly common for subscription vendors to lose money in the first few months (or longer) of involvement with a new subscriber. These customers have to be on-boarded and trained, and only part of that cost comes from training and service fees; much of it is overhead. A new subscription customer that calls your service center is learning on your nickel because you are paying to staff the center. So if customers come and go at a rapid rate a vendor might not have time to recoup its investment in sales and onboarding. Slowing attrition is paramount in every subscription vendor's mindset.

There are many indicators that can provide a subscription vendor with advanced warning about customer intentions and satisfaction, such as active usage of your service. Another is more qualitative indicator is how often a customer checks into your service. If a customer is using your service heavily, there's a good correlation to satisfaction. Many subscription businesses, especially in the SaaS space, have organized teams around driving *customer success*. These teams proactively work with customers to ensure they're happy and using the service well. It positively impacts their businesses. When was the last time you encountered a conventional business-model company that was actively concerned about your success? It's quite common in the subscription industry.

Attrition is commonly thought of as a failure, regardless of the reason, to renew an annual contract. For planning purposes, it leaves a vendor with a hole in the budget. Do that enough times and you have a big problem. Attrition and churn are closely related but with churn the recurring revenue is assumed on a

42

monthly rather than an annual basis. In businesses where there are no annual contracts churn and attrition are the same, but with annual contracts attrition refers to losing a customer at the end of the contract, which is less random but still hurts.

Retention is the reciprocal of attrition and is measured as a percent of all customers capable of leaving who renew. The renewal rate for a healthy company will typically be over 90 percent so attrition will be under 10 percent and, yes, it's important to measure it.

You can get very fine grained in analyzing attrition and churn. Consider an end user company that uses three different subscription products across three divisions. Attrition can occur if one or more divisions reduce their uptake of a product, if a division completely drops out, or if the company fails to renew. The reasons for attrition and churn are myriad and smart companies find ways to measure uptake, use, and satisfaction in all possible ways.

"These measurements are important as indicators of whether your relationship with a customer is growing or shrinking," Tzuo says. "Sometimes the change is beyond your control, such as when a business is downsizing or exiting a line of business." Tzuo's bottom line: "Often it's a direct reflection of how well are you contributing value to their business." That's why subscription companies measure and analyze all the customer data that they can.

Recurring revenue (and recurring profit)

Recurring revenue (RR) can be measured monthly (MRR) or annually (ARR or ACV — annual contract value), and different calculations use each of these measures. Revenue that's from an existing customer is considered recurring and it's assumed to have fewer charges against it. Usually, the cost of things like onboarding the customer, including training and guidance through first use, has already been absorbed. This might not be strictly true but it's a good approximation aimed at describing the quality of the revenue. It implies that this revenue will be more profitable than the same revenue from a new customer in the first year of a subscription.

Revenue from new business is assumed to have some calls on it, such as onboarding costs, and it will not be as profitable, though over time new revenue becomes recurring. So, recurring profit is generated from recurring revenue and it might actually increase (even if a company doesn't add new subscribers), simply because overhead may trend down. Recurring profit will also increase if you get a better handle on reducing churn.

A company that's rapidly gaining and losing customers might have high revenues but if the mix has too high a ratio of new revenue to recurring revenue, the company won't be as profitable as one might like — if it is at all — and this will be reflected in earnings. That's why a single measurement like recurring revenue might be misleading. It's also why as a manager you need to have visibility into multiple business metrics.

Deferred revenue is also part of the recurring-revenue discussion. Typically, a vendor will only recognize revenue as it becomes due so that a 12-month contract paid in advance looks just like 12 one-month contracts and the revenue is recognized one month at a time. So, in a multiyear agreement only the current year's revenue is on the books ready to be recognized in twelve equal amounts. The remaining revenue, which is committed to by contract but not yet billed or received, is considered unbilled deferred revenue. If that revenue had been billed and was sitting in a bank account controlled by the vendor, it would simply be deferred revenue.

All this might sound needlessly technical, but it has a serious point. A vendor might give a bigger discount to a customer willing to pay the full subscription amount up front, for instance, or to commit to a multiyear agreement. At the same time, a vendor that has a good idea of the quantity of its recurring revenue will have an easier time accurately forecasting growth to investors. For example, a vendor that wants to grow 50 percent in a year but that has half of its ARR already committed or deferred has an easier time generating the necessary growth. This is very important for planning purposes.

Growth efficiency or the cost of acquiring customers and revenue

Everything that goes into generating new revenue (not recurring revenue), such as marketing activities, sales headcount and commissions, and on-boarding new customers, is a cost associated with acquiring revenue. Recurring revenue has a very low cost; generating net new revenue is relatively more expensive. That's why it matters where the revenue comes from and why a high churn rate is so bad for the bottom line. So, a smart vendor will closely watch the cost of acquiring customers (CAC) along with other metrics. Ideally, that number will be low or at least trending downward. Of course, a company with zero customer-acquisition costs might also be stagnant — it's important to know what the CAC might look like if no net new revenue is coming in but the company is still paying for sales salaries, etc. This threshold is to be avoided as much as an excessively high CAC is, therefore a good management team will guide its company between the two extremes, close to a level that is optimal for the company's goals.

Other Subscription Metrics

We understand from all of this that subscriptions can vary over time in many different ways. Fortunately, everything that can fluctuate can be measured, and the wise manager keeps an eye on a variety of metrics and understands their ups and downs. The more data a vendor can collect and analyze about customer patterns, the better. Subscriptions offer the vendor many advantages, but especially in the area of metrics: Much of the most useful and interesting things a vendor can learn about a subscriber come from data that a vendor already almost certainly collects. When correctly analyzed, data turns into information and information drives the knowledge a vendor needs to make good decisions. Ideally, a manager will find some of the information generated this way to be diagnostic of the business and will consider it a metric or even a key performance indicator (KPI). Any metric should have the following four attributes:

1. It comes from credible data. The data used to derive the metric should come from a trusted source with

minimal effort. This includes customer-use data, customer demographics, revenue, and more.

2. It comes from simple calculation and transparency. A metric should be easily calculated and easy to understand. All the subscription metrics I've discussed fit this need and most are simple ratios.

3. It comes from easy, unambiguous interpretation. For instance, churn means something different from attrition, though they have a common root. When churn is up it means paying attention to short-term sales and marketing, service levels, and the on-boarding process. When attrition is up it signals that a company's offerings, including services and policies, may need review.

4. It is actionable. You can easily figure out what to do when presented with a given value for a metric, especially if you have data from several reporting periods to compare — is it going up or down and is that good or bad?

Many if not most subscription metrics (but not all sentiment metrics) can be derived from the vendor's financial data. Is revenue up or down? Why? Are the number of customers, their uptake of services, and revenue from their activities up or down? Are the number of products in use overall up or down and are the number of products in use by a particular customer up or down? How does this class of new customers compare with the new class from a year ago? Other financial metrics might include customer-lifetime value or value remaining, which are simple calculations based on a company's experience with various classes of customers.

Metrics that don't come directly from the financial data might come from user data. For instance, suppose your company supplies baby clothing by subscription and your target audience is parents of children from birth to two years old. There's a lot you can know about your customers and their likelihood of churning from their use data. For example, you can start a clock running when the parents sign up for the service and simply count out the next twenty-four months. You can do the same for sizes — perhaps a fast-growing baby will outstrip your product line sooner than an average one. You might also discover that you have more success with parents of one gender or the other. You can collect all of the data you need to discover the metrics that best enable you to forecast not only revenue, but also normal attrition (the kind that can't be helped, such as babies becoming toddlers).

By tracking use and financial data you can learn a great deal more about customers than whether or not their accounts are current. You can also discover some of their preferences and learn how well your products and services match their needs. For a children's clothing-subscription company that loses an inordinate number of customers after one year rather than two, perhaps it's early warning that customers don't like something about the selection or pricing. This tracking should give the manager the needed insight to investigate further.

What's Good for the Customer Is Good for the Bottom Line

This short course in subscription business-model metrics shows how important it is to keep customers, and keep them happy. Happy customers stay a long time and are relatively low maintenance once they are established, and so, are more profitable. In a traditional transaction setting, the revenue from a transaction can be big and customer happiness can be treated as a separate issue, but it may, in fact, never come up. In a subscription model the transaction and the delight are inseparable.

Every time a subscription customer picks up a phone to call a vendor or goes online to visit a vendor's site presents an opportunity for the vendor to earn the customer's recommitment — to build a bond. It is a moment of truth, which I cover in depth in Chapter 4.

A traditional vendor might be able to sell to a large number of customers. If some or many of them become unhappy, the vendor can continue to get by because that vendor collected a large fee all at once.

In a subscription model, each transaction is necessarily small and the revenue from the lifecycle only shows up one month at a time; therefore, the cost of acquiring new revenue makes customer retention essential — if you want to grow, you don't want to repeatedly spend on acquiring the same revenue. Companies that alienate customers at high rates will lose many of them and the cost of replacing them will make these businesses unprofitable. That's why subscriptions have turned the business world on its head and put the customer in the driver's seat again. It's also why the subscription model has a kind of gravity that enlists customers in a way of thinking that affects even traditional non-subscription companies.

You're on an equal footing now

Customers have more outlets than ever before to discuss their vendors and publicize their experiences — all of it. They can complain in public and they can trash your reputation for any reason or for no reason. Customers are now on equal footing with vendors and this is why the old manufacturing-era approach that treats all customers as interchangeable parts (while attempting to deal with them, as if dealing with them had some economy of scale), is over. Kaput.

Worse than trashing your reputation, many customers will simply leave vendors that are not meeting their needs. This is why proactively sifting through customer data trails has become so important for subscription companies — and now for any company.

The road ahead requires that vendors take account of customers and their activities. The only way to do this is to use automation to capture customer data and analyze it to uncover patterns that will influence the course of business. Managers must become adept at understanding the patterns, as well as at synthesizing the information from multiple sources and metrics into knowledge for better decision-making. Analytics holds the key to vendor success.

SftC Takeaways

1. Subscriptions are not just a delivery option. They make new modes of doing business possible.

2. Most important, they give customers options.

3. They also enable vendors to collect huge amounts of data about uptake and indications of satisfaction. This data underlies useful metrics you can use to manage the business and the customer.

Chapter 4 unpacks the customer lifecycle — even in subscriptions — and while it's not a mystery, it is vastly different from the traditional lifecycle that many companies are still wedded to.

Chapter Four

The Anna Karenina Principle and Moments of Truth

A company's business model should reflect its customer outlook, but in a specific way. The business model, at least the part that deals with customers, should be driven by Customer Science, an integrated approach to learning about customer needs and expectations and systematically crafting responses in unique moments of truth. Often moments of truth are a key difference between one-and-done transactions that reflect old-style business models and interactive models based on subscription principles. Adopting a Customer Science based approach to customers is a great way to tone down the antipathy in many markets and improve customer relationships. Customer Science has multiple parts, which the following chapters will explain, culminating in a consolidated description in Chapter 11.

There's an expectation mismatch in all this. Customers may require information, service, and many other things from vendors and the vendor ideal of speedy, one-and-done transactions with customers can be a real problem. The customer lifecycle has changed, regardless of business models or transaction orientation. We need to understand how and why customers behave as they do before we can begin to repair the vendor-customer split seen so often on sentiment sites.

Nobody expects perfection from a vendor aside from a few crazy people. Most people readily accept that companies make mistakes. But it's often not a mistake that drives customer discord; it's how companies handle the aftermath. Do they deny, ignore, stonewall, or act oblivious? Or do they go old school with the determination that customers need them and there's nothing more sacred than being there for the customer? The sentiment examples in Chapter 2 are mostly about processes gone badly and customers' reactions when they discover that they are stuck with few good alternatives. Those sentiments represent transactions that were served up as processes, causing frustration and anger.

There's a fundamental theory for understanding why great companies using modern technology go old school. After you come to understand it, you'll never look at a transaction again without searching for the underlying process.

The Anna Karenina Principle

There is no organization on earth without its detractors. Oil companies, software companies, car companies, banks and financial institutions, Ivy League colleges, airlines, churches — they all get their fair share of abuse in the Democratic Republic of the Internet. Not surprisingly though, sentiment is not homogeneous. Some entities are universally loved and others are pariahs. Even within markets that have predominantly high or low sentiment there are outliers, examples of companies that buck the trend. This is good because it shows that customers are not a bunch of implacable whiners. They are discerning and they reward or penalize vendors along parameters that make sense to them. They also care enough to offer feedback.

Leo Tolstoy's masterpiece *Anna Karenina* is a model for the importance of process in everyday life. It begins with the line, "Happy families are all alike; every unhappy family is unhappy in its own way." If we apply that declaration to the lives of real people in customer-vendor relationships, we have to wonder if it's ever possible to achieve a zero-defect state in which all customers are happy with a vendor. The answer is *no*, definitely not. But that shouldn't keep us from trying. If customers hate vendors after they've tried their mightiest to figure out how to help their customers, then their hate ought to be a badge of honor.

But it's important to understand that happy families are not happy because everything always goes right for them. They all have their

51

share of troubles and challenges. The difference between happy families and unhappy ones is that happy families know how to work through problem situations to reasonable outcomes. In business, happy customers are happy not because they are always lucky enough to get what they need, but because vendors work to make them so, especially when things go wrong. Vendors create happy customers when they deploy systems that not only accomplish transactions, but also mediate the processes that lead to transactions far better than the simple transaction systems that leave customers with no alternative other than to report something to a sentiment site.

Tolstoy's novel and the happy families idea has given name to the Anna Karenina Principle[1] (AKP), referring to any endeavor (a business endeavor, for our purposes) in which a deficiency of any factor in a relationship cascade can doom the effort. That's what a healthy relationships is, a cascade of events in which the vendor and customer achieve some form of accommodation. Kennedy School of Government chair and executive-education program lecturer Bob Behn writes[2] regarding the AKP that, "A family has to solve a large number of complex problems: How does the family deal with money, with children? How does it divide up the family's responsibilities? How does it manage the pressures of employment? If a family fails to handle any one of the many problems that all families must inherently face, it will be unhappy."

But if you want a happy family, you can't pick and choose which issues you want to deal with while ignoring the rest. Everything has to be solved at once because everything comes at you at once. We sometimes forget this in business, and instead try to isolate just one or two issues to work on at a time. For instance, if your bonus depends on increasing revenues, you might work on revenue generation (Sell! Sell! Sell!) to the exclusion of things like customer satisfaction. Someone else in your organization may be charged with satisfaction and at times you may work at cross-purposes. Without an overarching principle to guide both parties, neither one will achieve all its goals. Customers (or the balance sheet) may suffer as a result.

In business a cascade of events or a customer-facing process is predictable in that, for example, there only may be so many ways that you can sell a product or onboard a customer (although the process might have a few branches). These cascades comprise moments of truth, points in processes when the vendor must deliver on some aspect of the brand promise. Keep in mind that the brand promise is not solely what the vendor says. It's also the accumulation of customer expectations — as a vendor you have to keep up with these customer inflection points.

The customer lifecycle

Moments of truth are spread throughout the customer lifecycle and they are different for each company, industry, sector, and approach to the marketplace. There are six stages in the customer lifecycle today and each has multiple moments of truth you need to uncover in your business. Some people would say there are more stages, some would say fewer — some variability (based on the facts on the ground) is fine. The important thing is to stay faithful to your model, unless you later realize it's wrong. Your lifecycle model will be the foundation for other things like understanding your moments of truth, which we will see are critical building blocks for customer outreach. Let's look at these six phases and do some analysis.

Discovery

Discovery is an almost entirely customer-driven process that identifies a need and then a solution that fulfills that need, but understanding moments of truth can give you greater visibility even at this early stage. Asking what happens *before* discovery is like asking what happened before the Big Bang — it's a mystery. In the beginning we're happy creatures minding our business, not realizing there is something that we need to make our personal or business lives complete. Usually this involves finding a small list of products or vendors that fit the need (at least approximately). Then it's off to the evaluation.

Evaluation

Some evaluation has to happen whether you intend to buy a solution online or through a conventional sales process involving retail stores or professional salespeople. You have to weed out what you don't want and to settle on what you can afford.

Today customers perform discovery and, depending on the product, do much or most of their evaluation independent of a store environment or the charms of a salesperson. This gives most vendors heartburn. In the recent past vendors controlled information flow: If you wanted to know about a solution you had to talk to the vendor, its representatives, or a store associate. It took time to set up meetings, go to the meeting, take notes, and, have your horizons limited to a couple of choices to make the decision quick and easy — for the vendor. That was fun, wasn't it? Today, with much of discovery and evaluation happening off a vendor's radar, it's understandable that they might be a little uptight about procedure. No heroic attempts at controlling process are going to change this, but understanding moments of truth might.

Purchase

Everyone loves purchase. Vendors love it because it brings in revenue and puts another unit into the world. Customers love it because it satisfies a need, to say nothing of the tiny bit of dopamine (a pleasure hormone), released into the brain of a buyer. (Shopping malls are at their essence, like drug stores, in my humble opinion.) Everyone gets a little high on a purchase, and people need to make another purchase soon after the first to keep the dopamine flowing. For a merchant, a purchase is a milestone. It's the point at which most vendors begin to earn their keep.

Use/experience

The bliss of purchase is followed by the joy of use and knowing that you now have a solution to that problem that surfaced the last time you were happy. The first-use experience is a tricky time. It often involves a learning curve for the customer. Smart vendors learned long ago to do everything they could to provide customers a positive first experience. They built customer service centers and hot lines, and many also built websites and other online aids to get new customers on board and over the first-use hump as quickly and effortlessly as possible. Most customers quickly wean themselves from vendor support and become happily engaged with their products. They may even brag to others about the great deal they got on a swell purchase.

Bond

Happily engaged customers bond with their products and then their vendors. This is important: A bonded customer is more likely to contribute to a positive NPS for the vendor, product, or even the brand. If vendors miss this bonding step, it can lead to a big-time failure that might land them on some of the sucks and sentiment sites listed in Chapter 2.

While bonding might be listed as a phase in the lifecycle, this can be deceiving because customers don't bond all at once. Bonding is the accumulation of positive experiences that can come either directly with experience of the product or service, or from the satisfaction of having a problem taken care of promptly for instance. So failure to bond goes back farther in the cascade to the many things that customers expect in their moments of truth that a vendor may have failed to deliver. And, every unbonded customer is unbonded for different reasons.

Failing to bond is a break in a cascade that too often results in the wheels falling off the advocacy wagon.

Advocate

Happy customers are all alike: They got as far as they did unscathed sometimes by luck but other times through dint of a vendor's perseverance. So, customers become advocates (to one degree or another). They're alike because everything that could go wrong in the discovery, evaluation, purchase, use, and bonding phases didn't or because failures were detected and repaired before they caused lasting damage. Because it's a lifecycle, nothing ends when you get to the advocate stage; instead, advocates help recruit the next wave of new customers through word of mouth, or word of social — better yet, they buy more. The paradox is that when it all works it's completely undetectable at sentiment sites.

If you don't have a large number of customers that go on to become advocates for your company or brand, you need to go back to each of the lifecycle phases and ask your customers what you can do to secure their advocacy. Don't ask your staff members unless they talk frequently and consistently to customers: Non-customer-facing feedback is opinion, not engaged-customer user-experience, which is what you want to improve.

Bonding: The New Imperative

Traditional customer approaches that relied on transactions and trading products for cash were really good for working through the first half of the lifecycle. A typical company with a reasonably aggressive and well-paid sales staff always nailed the discovery, evaluation, and purchase parts of the lifecycle. A few years ago you may even have taken a serious interest in loving your customers, making sure their first and subsequent use experiences with your product were top notch. You made sure all the green lights were flashing on whatever you sold before you handed in the final bill. Maybe you even bolstered your customer-service group — boy, was that expensive! But soon you found ways to automate some key parts of sales and service, thus reducing your costs and improving profitability. So, what went wrong?

Unfortunately, your involvement in the first part of the lifecycle is shrinking. You no longer know who has a need or who's interested in a specific product until the customer is in a purchase process. At that point, all you can do is present, propose, and pray. That's no way to feel good about your sales forecast.

If your window of opportunity for influencing the buying process has narrowed significantly, it also has opened wide for your existing, bonded customers to do some advocacy work. Your bonded customers are the natural advocates for your company, products, and brand. Bonding and advocacy are the two big business issues that we have to consider today.

It's easy to see through the lens of the AKP that companies struggling with their customers have failed in one or more ways to promote satisfactory bonding. Bonding happens when customers receive value and validation. Value comes in the form of delivering the product or service that was purchased in a timely manner and validation happens when the customer confirms the value. In AKP terms the necessary processes ran to completion, and moments of truth were successful — even if the process needed human assistance.

Analyzing the lifecycle this way can help pinpoint where most of the things that the AKP hints at occur. Your customers already have your product: One way or another they've gotten through the first three or four parts of the lifecycle. If customers aren't bonded, the trouble lies upstream — it's a matter of collecting and analyzing data to figure out where and then to improve your processes.

But you can never discount the idea that some of your customers might be there for the wrong reasons. For instance, maybe they didn't need all the functionality you offered and would have been satisfied with a less expensive product. Or maybe they ran out of money midway through implementation and couldn't do the training and deployment right, which had lingering consequences. Remember, "...every unhappy family is unhappy in its own way."

How to fail at bonding

There are two ways to fail at bonding. Either you never bond — a distinct possibility, especially if you're mired in a pure transaction situation — or you fall out of a bond because of a misunderstanding (or plain old bad service). United Breaks Guitars and the Comcast class action had elements of both. It's very hard to see the moment of dissatisfaction or disappointment (that point in time when a bond was broken or damaged), because today so many customer-facing business processes have been automated. You can easily monitor the aftereffects of the damage at sites like the PissedConsumer.com but by then it's too late.

Some analysts will tell you it's all because you haven't completely figured out the customer experience. I don't disagree, but I think that explanation is a little too broad. Very often the customer experience people talk about involves engineering the way they interact during the sales process. Although that's part of the customer experience, it's not enough to foster customer bonding. In a business world heavily influenced by subscriptions, the sales process is no longer the lifecycle.

Back when your product category was new and everyone needed it, you could easily get away with engineering the sales-and-use parts of the customer experience and all would be well. Customers were just looking for well-priced functionality, not a whole product. But over time we see product definition creep. Customers demand more and more in the classification of well-priced functionality until they're demanding something approaching a full product delivered throughout a full customer lifecycle replete with reasonable policies and empathy.

With this insidious creep, many vendors suddenly discover they can't compete. They find themselves in a different country that speaks a language they don't understand. In large industries like banking, cable, telephone service, or air transport, for example, the product or service more or less commoditizes and succumbs to lowest common denominator thinking. At the same time, automation tries to make customer interactions cookbook easy because vendors are watching costs like a dog at a pig roast. Vendors do enough to provide service, keep attrition manageable, and keep regulators off their backs, but in a commoditized market there hasn't been room in the fee structure to pay for customer bonding — until now. As a result, sentiment sites do a thriving business as do all those other sites on which customers liberally employ earthy Anglo-Saxon words to describe you.

A vendor's limits to growth are rarely related to market size. The limit to a vendor's continuing success is its ability to re-access the market, especially in large ones where vendors who have mastered the art of introducing new products and cross- or upselling customers who have bought before. That limit is based on customer bonding, advocacy, and the trust a customer places in a vendor.

When a vendor's business model is strictly oriented towards accumulating market share, it might indicate a classic new-category situation in which a new vendor is selling a relatively vanilla product into a new market or that the vendor has a very limited number of products to offer and expects nothing more than a one-time sale. Today these situations only clear the way for competitors to disrupt the original vendor as customers seek better policies and practices and with more complete product offerings — the customers seek a replacement vendor that is unlike the first.

It's easy to blame the collapse of the vendor-customer relationship on communication failures, but it actually signals an earlier breakdown that can best be described as a missed opportunity: a moment of truth between the vendor and customer. Multiplied many times, missed moments of truth can spell disaster.

Customer Lifecycle: Cascading Moments Of Truth

All vendor-customer relationships have moments of truth, points in time when vendors have to come through with a combination of product, service, or empathy for the customer condition. Moments of truth are common and predictable. For example, having a robust service process that doesn't keep customers waiting or having ample employee training on how to onboard new customers. Moments of truth require employee empowerment and planning, but they should be limited and should reflect things that a vendor decides to offer as an expertise that customers desire. These things should be reflected in the product offering and the company business model.

Advancements in quality engineering, better manufacturing techniques, digital reliability, and the enhanced importance of design have combined over the past several decades to produce an environment in which vendors do their best to assure satisfaction with products and services by eliminating moments of truth. Intuitive, easy-to-use products are good ideas but no vendor can say that it has engineered away all the moments of truth when customers require vendor involvement. So without escalation procedures for dealing with customer issues that can pop up at any time, even the intuitive products become brittle. Your whole product is only as good as the processes you surround it with.

The focus on moments of truth is fleeting in many situations and is offered primarily in the sales process. Failing to maintain attention throughout the customer lifecycle can reduce the amount of bonding that customers do with a brand or a vendor.

And just when a vendor needs the benefits of bonding — during customer referral — the bonds are not strong enough to make the critical difference.

When things go bad between a vendor and a customer the situation can quickly become a major event involving people with little interest in a dispute. A dispute often is less about a product than concerns over policies, procedures, and business practices — i.e., whole products in moments of truth. The results of the dispute are misaligned expectations, especially when customers deal with impersonal systems or with functionaries who are not empowered to solve problems.

Comcast's fast-growth business practices put it at odds with its customers, who were accustomed to stable prices from similar-looking utility services; when they realized they had few alternatives, they responded with a class action suit. United fell back on its rigid rules and didn't empower its personnel to deal authentically with Dave Carroll in his moment of truth — a failure the carrier could have foreseen in some of its business practices (and which may have been exacerbated by aging computer systems).

Each situation that results in customers becoming angry enough to take significant action against a vendor is the result of multiple missed moments of truth (and opportunities). The vendor was tested by circumstance and found wanting. Moments of truth are common and they can even be the reason we select our vendors during a sales process. A customer buys a solution *because it satisfies* a moment of truth.

Customers look for vendors that are adept at solving customer challenges. These are moments of truth that form initial vendor-customer bonds. But like a game of Whac-A-Mole, once one problem is solved another can soon pop up — a fresh moment of truth that the vendor may not handle well, perhaps one the vendor failed to plan for. Customers then might discover their vendors are not proficient at improvising during a moment of truth or of showing empathy. That was part of Dave Carroll's problem with United, which stemmed from tight procedures that left employees with no flexibility to act.

Of course, these situations represent poor customer experiences but part of managing the customer experience is keeping the customer "happy." But too often vendors wait for customers to define what happiness is. Rather than trying to model moments of truth in advance, some vendors try to be all things to all people. That is an impossible goal.

Smart vendors define in advance what happiness is, and decide what they can deliver and what is outside of their scope and they communicate this to customers. This helps to define moments of truth that their employees can turn into memorable customer interactions, rather than simply providing a product or service.

A customer experience inevitably becomes a decision point for a vendor about how to take action that will meet all of a customer's expectations about the encounter. On the customer side of a moment of truth, each time a customer engages in one of these moments, it is an evaluation point at which the customer assesses a vendor's performance. One missed moment of truth might not damage the relationship but repeated misses result in inadequate bond formation and all that goes with it.

Again, many companies, especially product companies, work very hard to engineer moments of truth from of their products. Apple champions the idea that products should be intuitive and easy to figure out — that idea is a way of removing the possibility of negative moments of truth.

Removing what can go wrong at the product level is a great way of removing frustration. But what about the whole product level, which involves processes, procedures, and policies? Customer-facing business processes, unlike products, don't always lend themselves to simplification. Even if they do, is it ever possible to think of all of the ways a process can go off the rails and require direct assistance?

Empathy in moments of truth

Diane Hessan is the chairman of Communispace (a subsidiary of Omnicom), a company dedicated to helping companies engage with their customers through social-media communities. She's the coauthor of *Customer Centered Growth: Five Proven Strategies for Building Competitive Advantage*,[3] and she's been a student of customer interactions since her days at Harvard Business School. Through the Internet, Communispace helps major brands by enlisting target people into communities to provide insights and advice on a wide variety of issues that are important for growth and innovation. Companies use the information from their custom Communispace communities to improve products and services as well as their business processes.

Not surprisingly, Hessan refers to customer interactions as moments of truth. In a wide-ranging interview with me for *Solve for the Customer*, she discusses customer-oriented business processes and gives some surprising insights. For instance, Hessan thinks frequency can be a big differentiator and not always in a positive way. In the airline industry, for instance, she says, "I think the problem with the airlines is that there are just too many moments of truth."

Compared to banks, airlines have their work cut out for them. Hessan says: "What's your moment of truth like with a bank? You get online, you pay your bills, and you get off. Or you go to an ATM machine and you get out. If you have a problem, you pick up the phone and call. How many times do you have to interact with that bank over a year? Fifty? One hundred?"

But with an airline, you could have that many moments of truth in just one trip! "You probably have 50 moments of truth on one complicated flight — from the time you're buying your ticket and all the things that go with that to picking your seat to figuring out your baggage to making all of those decisions about whether you want this kind of insurance or that kind of insurance to every single possibility of what could go wrong at the airport. Then there's the flight, and then when you get off and when you get billed and when you see if you got your frequent flyer points. There are just so many opportunities for an airline to mess up."

Of course, this is the light version of reality. Security screening, seat size (Do you want to purchase extra room for your femurs?), and the boarding process also present their own moments of truth.

But Hessan's summary leaves little doubt. "When there are that many interactions you just can't automate all the solutions. You have to have people that get it." And even more to the point, she adds, "Having people requires you to have a culture that's special and that matters, where people feel proud of the organization. Then, if your culture is good, your quality is good — and vice versa."

That's a tall order.

But every aspect of a successful company-customer interface need not be a moment of truth. What company could measure up if every situation were? Moments of truth are the situations that companies choose to be competitive in. A luxury car company might choose to be competitive on customer service, while a low-end brand might tout reliability because it has removed as many possibilities of failure as possible to make customer service a less critical issue. Hessan says, "You've got to pick what you're going to be great at and what you're not going to worry about."

And how do you pick those things? "I don't know how you pick that without empathy. Institutional, formal empathy — capital E — for and with your customers."

What Hessan describes is anything but guessing and it often requires detailed analysis, which is why it's important to develop a community of like-minded people who will volunteer their ideas about how a company can identify its moments of truth and improve.

Vendors have tried to guess what customers want for almost as long as people have conducted commerce. Sometimes the results have been impressive and an intuition hit the target, but more often guesses have missed the mark and resulted in lost opportunity, lost revenue, and maybe lost customers. As Nate Silver writes in *The Signal and the Noise: Why So Many Predictions Fail-but Some Don't*, "We need to stop and admit it: we have a prediction problem. We love to predict things — and we aren't very good at it."[4]

Getting to why

Big data is one of the dominant approaches to better understanding customers today. Companies capture enormous quantities of customer data, from mouse clicks and purchase data to how customers use various products and services. The typical approach to using all this data is to analyze it using powerful software that can identify patterns and trends. As valuable as this approach is, it is often not enough because it only answers questions about what the customer is, does, or thinks. That doesn't make a relationship or provide opportunities to develop empathy.

"I think the Holy Grail of relationships is less about understanding what customers do and more focusing on why they do it," Hessan says. Indeed, understanding why customers think and behave as they do can help a company determine how to treat them. This requires a different approach, one that seeks to build relationships rather than one that simply seeks to capture data for analysis. That approach will give you a bell curve distribution for most things you study, but then you might realize that few if any customers fit the mean of the curve that you've developed. So, the difference between building relationships and doing data analysis is subtle and you need both to get at the "what" and the "why" of customers.

Getting to why comes down to listening and the result of listening may be to identify the right one or two qualities that customers attribute to their vendors. For this you have to directly ask the customer. As Hessan says, "Once they understand that on the other side of the computer screen it really is you listening, and once they trust that their opinion is going to matter, they're going to tell you stuff that they've never told anybody."

"Our system won't let us do that."

The situation many vendors find themselves in regarding customers typically is self-imposed by conducting business as usual year in and year out. Standing pat was once a good strategy when nothing much changed. Companies used a manufacturing business model that sourced materials, built products, sold them and collected the money. They built systems that supported the model but then the music stopped and many vendors found that there weren't enough chairs. Business and customers today require different thinking, and vendors can't do so at their leisure. The Comcast and United examples are only two of the most obvious in a confrontation that is just heating up.

Many customer-facing computer systems in place at numerous corporations right now were deployed in the 1990s and 2000s for very different business environments from what we have today. In the 1990s, many corporations rebuilt their back-office accounting systems or bought new enterprise resource planning (ERP) systems in anticipation of the turn of the century. These systems were oriented toward manufacturing and were designed to keep track of money and raw materials (and their flows) as well as finished goods. ERP was and is the system of record for many companies that need to know what they've produced, who owes them money, and to whom they owe money.

At the same time CRM became the software that helped turn a bunch of disparate, manual front office-business processes into repeatable and traceable operations. Sales, marketing, and customer service were consolidated into CRM and later, much of social media joined the group. We're still working on turning the manual processes into repeatable operations, in part because unlike manufacturing (where there is a limited number of processes), in the front office customers can randomly dictate what companies do, at least before the sale. But just like manufacturing, it will take dedication to the idea of continuous improvement driven by data analysis to improve customer-facing processes.

Implementing the first ERP and CRM systems was difficult, expensive, and took years for some companies (and in some cases nearly ruined the companies they were designed to help). The bad experiences from early CRM implementation projects echo around the software industry. Few people in the IT industry have forgotten those implementations and no one wants to relive those times. Consequently, many CRM users are leery of even incrementally changing their systems. So the systems don't keep up with changes in business and become brittle.

But most software vendors today have gone out of their way to create systems that are easier to deploy and use. They've both simplified and made their products more robust, while they've contained the costs and the effort required for deployment.

And failure to adapt is not only bad for customers (although they feel the effects directly), but it also impedes the long-term success of the enterprise. If you've ever heard someone from IT or finance say, "Our system won't let us do that," it probably means, *We can't go into that line of business profitably even though we see there is a business need or demand.* It might also be shorthand for *our ancient systems can't accommodate a simple change to a modern business process.*

People, Process, and Technology

So how does a company take itself from its 20th century model of selling products (rather than services) in one-and-done transactions to making itself a business dedicated to customers, selling products as recurring services and intuiting customer demand from data trails? Companies starting out can easily pick the new model and build their businesses accordingly. Established companies can convert one part of the business at a time through actions like capturing customer input and using it as the basis for future product and policy decisions.

Advances in IT always have centered on PPT. These three ingredients of success were so well known that they became a mantra — then we stopped paying attention to it. People became impediments to success as a wave of self-service strategies took hold. People became something an enterprise had too much of, while automation was supposed to enable the enterprise to automate manual processes and run leaner and more profitably.

As technology was in the ascent, normal business processes that were once mediated by employees, who could use their common sense, were replaced by transaction systems that could speed up front-office processes but not necessarily take responsibility for customer satisfaction.

SftC Takeaways

1. Customer Science begins with understanding moments of truth. We collect and analyze data from moments of truth to drive modern vendor-customer interactions.

2. Today's customer lifecycle is made up of moments of truth. The Anna Karenina Principle helps orient you towards business models built around moments of truth.

3. Customer bonding happens in moments of truth throughout the lifecycle. If you expect that bonding is a discrete part of the lifecycle you will be disappointed.

The pendulum has already begun to swing back to the center, a place where average people using smart systems enhance customer-facing processes so that enterprise costs remain low while customer satisfaction rises again. Next, in Chapter 5, we turn our attention to the people who work for us. When we empower them, they make magic.

Chapter Five

Use Good Judgment

We've used people, process, and technology as shorthand for how to successfully implement and use business software systems for a long time and while they are essential elements of Customer Science, they are not the science itself. Customer Science is about how we use all CRM elements in concert but it also involves a few newer technologies that many have not embraced yet. Still it's critical to review our PPTs for the simple reason that in some businesses over emphasis on one element and the declining importance of others has created an imbalance in customer outreach. This chapter explores the importance of people even at a time when automation continues to reduce the absolute need for employees in many customer-facing processes.

People oversee processes

What do today's customers want? CRM evidence suggests that they want to be in control, to get what they want when, where, and how they want it, and that they are not likely to wait for a vendor to decide how much information to share with them. Customers now have many kinds of resources, including social media, big data, and analytics, and are increasingly sophisticated about how to use these tools.

We thought just a few years ago that we knew what kinds of engagement and experiences customers seek. Stories about American Girl and its shopping experience enthralled us in the 1990s (Tea parties with girls' dolls as guests!). It was the epitome of mingling product and service as an advanced form of customer experience. Many vendors rushed to adapt the American Girl model to their businesses.

And think of Starbucks, with its ambiance, lighting, comfy chairs, Wi-Fi, and custom-made beverages. What is Starbucks if not a highly refined product and service rolled into one experience? Customers love it, but the coffeehouse model isn't for everyone. Sometimes you just need a cup of coffee for the road.

These companies' product, service, and experience ideas aren't wrong, but they are incomplete. Thousands of companies strive to provide an enhanced experience for their customers and it occasionally misfires. If these efforts are on target, most of the time it's because the models overlap with the fundamental customer need.

So, what *is* the basic customer need? Customers need and want competent, well-executed, timely processes. The Starbucks experience and the American Girl tea parties are great examples of these processes, just as Comcast and United's strategies are examples of what not to do.

Starbucks, American Girl, and many other companies are good examples of how to deliver timely processes and like happy families these companies are alike because they understand the value of asking their customers what they need and of marshaling PPT to achieve the necessary results. That's a very different approach to the customer experience.

Customer experience

Customer experience isn't what it once was and that's a good thing. We use the term as a noun in CRM (i.e., *the* customer experience), and for a long time it *has* been a noun. But once we begin to think in terms of customer-facing processes situated around a moment of truth, *experience* becomes a verb: You *experience* the moment of truth. That's an important difference and one that significantly helps vendors and customers.

A customer's experience (noun) is subjective and when you consider the multitude of customers and the totality of their experiences, you are dealing with a big number. More important, because all these experiences are subjective they are also unique — there are billions and billions of them. With so many unique experiences you can see that dealing with them or trying to build software to accommodate them is impossible.

But when you take a moments-of-truth approach, the customer's experience becomes a manageable problem. True, the experience is still subjective and customers are still unique. But there's a limited number of moments of truth in your business and with your products, which your customers will be glad to verify, and these moments of truth are linked in cascades governed by the Anna Karenina Principle.

Best of all, succeeding in a moment of truth and successfully navigating a cascade is Boolean — on or off, up or down, true or false, it worked or it didn't. If it all works you have a happy customer; if the moment of truth doesn't work and the cascade gets broken, you can pinpoint the problem and know exactly what to do to make it right. As a matter of fact, you can develop contingency plans in advance for all of the things that could go sideways. Of course you'd do this in your journey builder application, which brings up the need for a multifaceted software platform that we'll look at in Chapter 11.

When we talk about how a customer experiences (verb) a moment of truth we are at once simplifying the problem and escalating the customer experience to be something that we can act on. It also means there will be many times when we need to position our people in those moments, times when automation alone might not cut it.

Algorithms and processes

We love algorithms, business rules, those quasimathematical bits of logic that say, "If this, then do that." They run our personal lives in ways of which we are scarcely aware: If it's six o'clock, I turn on the news; I never/always eat chocolate when it's offered. In business an algorithm is often mediated by software systems. Algorithms increasingly are coming to replace people in critical points of business processes. For instance, you can apply for a loan or a mortgage online without ever speaking to a loan officer. Just fill out a form and an algorithmically driven program will crunch through your data, score it, and reduce it all to a yes-or-no answer that determines whether or not you get the loan. Only then you might have to talk to someone. But what if the form misbehaves?

Gray-area responses may be forwarded to a person to perform further analysis, but not always.

Algorithms have become increasingly powerful in a matter of a few years, thanks to brute-force data crunching. They will gain even greater capabilities over time. Machines like IBM's Watson and the Google Self-Driving Car produce amazing results. You might believe they're thinking, but they aren't. Watson beat some of the best *Jeopardy!* players in the world because it had more than 200 million pages of information loaded into it plus some snappy algorithms that enabled it to quickly sort through the data and calculate probabilities for its answers. It then submitted the highest probability answer; it wasn't always right, but was often enough to outplay the humans.

Chess grandmaster Garry Kasparov beat IBM's Deep Blue (an earlier version of Watson) in 1996 by literally out thinking it. Every possible move in chess is documented somewhere and it was logical to expect that IBM would ensure that Deep Blue had all of that information at its disposal for the match between its computer and the grand master. So Kasparov did something clever: He changed his process by inventing new openings for his game so that the computer would not be able to use its prodigious memory and would need to rely on its algorithms. Predictably the machine stumbled and Kasparov won the match though a year later the tables were turned. Today, sophisticated algorithms and better computers make the incident look quaint.

Kasparov showed that having great data crunching was not enough and his success strongly suggests that process plus human intervention were other critical components. People don't beat computers at chess any more but now they work together in tournaments. From this experience Kasparov developed an intriguing algorithm of his own that we can apply directly to business: Weak human + machine + better process was superior to a strong computer alone and, more remarkably, superior to a strong human + machine + inferior process.[1]

The Anna Karenina Principle precisely shows how process matters and there's plenty of evidence about the importance of technology. This leaves us with one more critical element in solving for the customer: people, which we'll se shortly.

Big data and analytics

The rise of the Internet, ecommerce, and social media has generated huge new pools of data about customers, including data about their preferences and behaviors. Analytics applied to this data is producing a trove of new information about demand in all its forms. Smart managers see this data (and the information it produces) not only as potential new knowledge about what to sell, but also as a tool for improving outreach to customers in marketing, sales, and service. Some of this new information can influence how a business' processes are carried out (and potentially inform new processes), when it's fed back into common business practice.

When manufacturers decided to collect data about production and finished products the result was a revolution in manufactured goods' quality. With better, more accurate feedback on the manufacturing process, quality and reliability improved and costs came down (in part, a consequence of lower waste and less rework).

The rise of front-office processes

Conventional customer-facing systems were built on some important assumptions (everyone needed your product and demand was always increasing), which may no longer be valid. Support for customer-facing processes centered on selling and servicing. Vendors needed accurate records for sales-and-support processes. In sales, it was enough to capture and hold on to demographic and deal-specific data. In service, data about product ownership, warranty, and service-level agreements covered most of the bases. It was all data but it turned into knowledge in the minds of the people who ran the relevant business processes. As long as there were people to convert data to knowledge the system worked.

But we've taken people out of our customer-facing processes as we've automated and economized. Worse, too often we've replaced smart people with (updated) dumb databases. This doesn't always result in happy customers, but there's a seed of a solution here. We can use our big data and analytics to winnow the real opportunities or cries for help and preserve the economies of scale automation provides, while improving our outreach and maybe even promoting bonding.

A workable solution

During the early part of the Information Age we invested heavily in technology to help people do their customer-facing jobs. That was good because process lived in people's heads. Reliance on technology made a great deal of sense when most business processes were manual and information's availability was bottlenecked. But we lost sight of the fact that manual processes were mediated by people whose brains can do magic with data, such as turning it into knowledge for decision-making.

Humans process many types of data, not just the kind stored in databases. For instance, the vibes given off by a customer standing in front of a sales person or talking on the phone with a service agent or even a tweet issued on the Internet are all types of data that humans excel at processing. You don't often need to tell a good service agent about a customer's sentiment. It's all over the customer's face and speech and the agent absorbs it unconsciously because doing so is a skill that's hard wired into humans.

Our reliance on information technology gave us a false sense that we could understand and deal with customers through automation but at some point we over relied on that resource with the results we see today. We took human understanding out of many business processes hoping that technology would replace them *and* boost profits. It did, but at the cost of excluding vendors and their personnel from many of the critical customer moments of truth.

We can't reverse course and go back to a pre-technological era of a purely human customer interface but we can do something better. We can appropriately pair technology with people in dynamic processes just as Kasparov observed. That's a key message in the pair of books by Erik Brynjolfsson and Andrew McAfee, professors at MIT's Sloan School of Management who wrote *Race Against the Machine*[2] and *The Second Machine Age*. They're fans of Kasparov, too, and according to them the most powerful force in business and life today is not a supercomputer or a smart person, it's combining a decent computer with appropriate software plus an average person engaged in a well-defined process. Process is where people and technology meet up to do good things — process is the nexus of decent computers with appropriate software and dedicated people.

Because the Anna Karenina Principle is the essence of process, we understand that that process must include not only the basic procedure but also the repair mechanisms that enable any process to branch around a dead spot. That's the basic idea of the Internet, a network of networks that would survive a nuclear attack. It's also the secret of DNA's resilience through billions of years. DNA can be damaged and disrupted but in many situations living things have evolved the mechanisms needed to repair breaks and continue life's processes. That should be our standard.

We've already looked closely at process. Let's turn our attention to people. You don't need to spend six figures on a consultancy to help you figure out your customer-facing processes. It starts with people and empathy, and includes a clear understanding of the goals and objectives of your business. A good example of how to leverage people in business today comes from inbound marketing-technology company HubSpot.

The HubSpot Story

MIT graduates Dharmesh Shah and Brian Halligan cofounded HubSpot in 2006 to produce inbound-marketing technology and a new approach to marketing. The company's SaaS offering helps businesses attract, engage, and delight customers on the web. Located in Cambridge, MA, near their old school, the company has more than 10,000 customers and has been listed twice on the Inc. 500. The company has also raised more than $100 million in venture capital, and in late 2014 it had its initial public offering. Shah and Halligan are the coauthors of *Inbound Marketing: Get Found Using Google, Social Media and Blogs*. The book was a runaway hit and has been translated into eight languages.

Shah also blogs at OnStartups.com,[3] which has more than 350,000 members in its online community. He's an active member of the Boston-area entrepreneurial community, an angel investor in more then 40 startups, and a frequent speaker on the topic of startups, company culture, and inbound marketing.

Dharmesh Shah, CTO

As is the case with most startups, for HubSpot there were many more jobs that needed doing than there were people to do them. The company decided to focus almost entirely on hiring people who GSD — get *stuff* done. Five years on, the company's executive team began thinking about how it could codify what made HubSpot's culture so special and how to leverage awareness of its culture to attract top candidates.

It was a challenge for two reasons. First, by the time the company got around to this bit of housekeeping, a corporate culture already had emerged, and second, the person heading up the project was Dharmesh Shah, who is HubSpot's CTO and a self-avowed introvert and non-people person.

Shah put his personal feelings aside, put on his engineer's hat, and analyzed the situation, taking nothing for granted. He asked numerous basic questions about his company and its employees. Once he'd collected a lot of data he analyzed it and came up with a blueprint for the way HubSpot and its people operated. It was a very successful effort, in part because there was already a kernel of a corporate culture that simply needed documenting, but also because what Shah uncovered is highly transferrable — and very relevant to our discussion.

Shah and Halligan are compulsively transparent, open, and honest about how their company operates and what it needs to do to continue to grow. The following section is taken from *Culture Code: Creating A Lovable Company*, a slide show[4] available on SlideShare that Shah developed. It summarizes his analysis of HubSpot's culture, and has inspired many other companies as they developed their own cultures. I am greatly indebted to Shah for speaking with me for *Solve for the Customer*. Please refer to the endnotes to learn more.

HubSpot's Culture Code

Business today is as much about sociology and other -ologies (the so-called soft sciences), as it is about accounting, finance, engineering, and manufacturing. And like a social science, business needs to answer *why* questions, much as Communispace's Hessan recommends (see Chapter 4). Shah asked why questions many, many times to develop the seven points that both define HubSpot's culture and drive its success. It is amazing how well they map to the AKP. The short version is here:

1. We are as maniacal about our metrics as our mission.
2. We Solve For The Customer (SFTC).
3. We are radically transparent.
4. We give ourselves the autonomy to be awesome.
5. We are unreasonably picky about our peers.
6. We invest in individual mastery and market value.
7. We constantly question the status quo.

HubSpot believes that great culture helps people deliver their best work, so why shouldn't a company, or any group, consciously try to build a culture they love and that works well for them?

Culture isn't static. It changes as people do, and it is generational. Consider how we've changed in the last couple of decades. Today people are driven to make money, sure, but having a job isn't enough as it might have been two decades ago. Today people also want meaning and or purpose in their work, and great colleagues to work with — that's partly culture. Technology has blurred the lines between private life and work life and today we can work whenever and wherever we choose. Many organizations haven't grasped either these elemental truths or the technologies that enable them, which makes solving for the customer more difficult.

In the recent past it was fine to hire average people to do an average job of following your business rules, but if you did that today you might find your company becoming average — reverting to the mean, as a statistician in the social sciences might say.

When you become average there's little compelling reason for customers to want to do business with you over a competitor. That's why it's so important to have a great culture that attracts amazing people. In Shah's formulation, culture is to recruiting as product is to marketing. "Customers are more easily attracted by a great product and amazing people are more easily attracted by a great culture," he says. Like all companies HubSpot is a work in progress and it always will be. The Culture Code emphasizes an important point emerging in business: the value of people.

In honor of Shah and HubSpot's delightfully quirky but workable Culture Code let's take a look at its major points in detail. Following is my review of these major points in order of importance to *Solve for the Customer*. Please note: I've kept Shah's original numbering.

2. We Solve For The Customer.

Solve For The Customer (SFTC) is Shah's succinct reduction of his analysis and chief imperative, "Solve for the customer, not just their happiness but their success." It's a math analogy used to make this point: The customer is a variable that must be solved for in an equation (i.e., a business process) with many expressions — that's practically a mathematical version of moments of truth. Shah says, "It's relatively easy to make customers happy. All you need to do is tell them what they want to hear and, in the short term at least, they'll be happy, though they might not be successful." Solving for the customer means doing both.

HubSpot's mission is to make the world of business more customer-centric; solving for the customer is the approach that works best for its customers. For instance, Shah and cofounder Halligan noticed that consumers had more tools than ever to block spam-y, interruptive advertising, yet companies and their marketing groups persisted in buying generic mailing lists and spending huge amounts of money on ads and other broadcast methods. The pair believed there was a better way to market, and created a software and service platform to make their vision a reality for more than 10,000 customers worldwide.

HubSpot believes that inbound marketing can help its customers achieve better relationships with their customers and improve revenues and profits. HubSpot's people seek to delight customers along that dimension. That's the primary moment of truth that HubSpot aims to cover. The question HubSpotters ask about every decision is, "What's in it for the customer?" That's where SFTC originates. It's business acumen that helps a company survive in the short term, so that it can delight customers in the long term. It's not magic, Shah says, it's "just the realization that bankrupt companies don't delight their customers."

It's also ample justification for making and hitting sales goals and a justification for finding and selling to customers that the company *expects to be able* to delight. HubSpot picks its customers the way it picks its employees, and why not? How does this compare with selling anything to anybody as long as it generates revenue? Knowing who you can and can't delight is as simple as understanding your potential customers' moments of truth. If a customer has a moment of truth that can't be satisfied by your existing model, why do the deal? It's bad business and writing bad business never made any company successful or loved, and HubSpot's culture positions the company to be loved.

4. We give ourselves the autonomy to be awesome.

How do they give themselves autonomy? Simple: They don't have a lot of rules. The prime directive — to borrow a phrase from *Star Trek* — is more like an algorithm that anyone can easily execute. HubSpot has a three-word policy on almost everything — Use Good Judgment. That's it. Whether it involves the sick-day policy, travel, social media, or buying a round of drinks at an event, the rule always is to use good judgment.

You might think that would get the company into hot water from time to time but it doesn't. HubSpot is picky about who it hires, so people who don't use good judgment are not a good fit for the culture and usually don't make it through the interview process. Shah explains the preference for a universal Use Good Judgment policy this way: "Just because someone made a mistake years ago doesn't mean we need a policy. We don't penalize the many for the mistakes of the few."

Not surprisingly, the company has a clear definition for what good judgment is in this context. It has three parts.

1. Favor your team over yourself.

2. Favor the company over the team.

3. Favor the customer over the company.

Why favor the customer over the company? Because acting in the customer's interest is acting in the long-term self-interest of the company. The long-term interest of the company is to delight customers, which includes a raft of corollary ideas that keep everyone focused.

Use good judgment also means adjusting your schedule to optimize your life and your contribution to the company. HubSpotters, like people in many emerging companies, work whenever, wherever but they also understand the importance of interacting. Part of the culture code is the belief that creative magic happens when quirky humans randomly connect — so much so that employees are required to change desks every 90 days to help foster new connections.

6. We invest in individual mastery and market value.

HubSpot believes in investing in people-capital in ways that benefit both the company and the individual. One small example: Want to read a book that might help your job? By using good judgment you can put in a request on the company Wiki and the ebook appears in your Kindle account. No drama, no expense reports.

5. We are unreasonably picky about our peers.

Deep in the culture is the assumption that amazing people with autonomy just act. They don't wait to be told, they don't overthink it, and they have a bias for action and like responsibility. It's summarized as JFDI, another important culture "codelet" — Just F*#king Do It. So with all this autonomy, what's a manager for? The culture code states, "Managers exist to help individual stars make magic." In fact, there are only two ways to be successful at HubSpot, either by making magic or by helping someone who is. HubSpot values people who are:

1. Humble: They're modest despite being awesome and they are self-aware and respectful. They share credit

when things are good and shoulder responsibility when things go sideways.

2. Effective: They're predisposed to act. They have a sense of ownership and they're resourceful and always looking for leverage.

3. Adaptable: They're constantly changing and learning. If you are good but looking for stability keep looking because change is constant at HubSpot — remember, every ninety days you change desks.

4. Remarkable: They have a certain *je ne sais quoi* and you'll know it when you meet them — they naturally stand out in one or more ways.

5. Transparent: They're open and honest with themselves and others.

There's a philosophy behind seeking these attributes in people. Shah likes to use the analogy of debt to illustrate his point. "A business takes on financial debt because it can use the cash productively *today*. The business knows that it will have to pay off that debt (with interest) at some point." Culture debt is similar. "You might hire someone who's not a perfect fit today," Shah says, "because you need someone to do a particular job (just like you might need cash)."

"What's important to recognize is that *you are incurring debt*," Shah says. And like any debt, the time to pay it will come. "My argument is, culture debt carries a relatively high interest rate — that a bad culture hire will certainly do the job in the short-term, but in the long-term bad culture hires reduce morale and cause you to drift from the culture you wanted to build. There comes a time that you have to pay the price for that short-cut taken."

Is the process perfect? No. And they don't always find people who score high on all five attributes. The attributes are aspirational — you've got to start somewhere. That's why they recognize that they really are unreasonably selective. After all, the people they hire will be both co-workers *and* the face of the company to the company's most important constituents: its customers.

1. We are maniacal about our mission and our metrics.

Now you have a sense of the mission, the attitude towards customers, and the company's approach to hiring its employees (and the expectation that they use good judgment). But how does HubSpot manage all this? With metrics, of course. Shah and Halligan are MIT grads so there's a built-in bias toward collecting and analyzing data about its business.

HubSpot understands that its metrics are what ultimately enables the company to earn the resources to further the mission of delighting customers. It's capitalism: Delight customers, earn profits, plow some of them back into the business, do it again. So, if something can be measured, Shah and Halligan measure it. Then, amazingly, they share it.

3. We are radically transparent.

Shah and Halligan believe that power is gained by sharing knowledge, so that's what they do with everyone in the company. They don't share every last bit of information, though. They protect information when it makes sense to, typically when it's required legally, such as information gained through a non-disclosure agreement (NDA) or when the information isn't completely theirs to share like individual compensation data.

The company's Wiki shares everything else: financials, board-meeting slides, strategic topics, company lore and mythology — all of it. And how do employees use the information? They use good judgment, of course.

7. We constantly question the status quo.

Entrepreneurs are all about disrupting the status quo, but as companies grow they become entrenched in their own disruption, which becomes the status quo. Shah and Halligan know that when this happens companies are in danger of reverting to the mean, so they question the status quo as part of their DNA.

Even more to the point HubSpot understands that you can't add simplicity in; you have to take complexity out. That's why it frequently looks for ways to refactor the company and its processes. Refactoring is a programmer's term for reviewing code and looking for ways to make it simpler and run a bit faster. It works in business processes, too. Refactoring is part of questioning.

Other ideas from Culture Code

When I started studying the Culture Code there were 10 points in the code but it's been refactored into seven. Here are a couple that are included by reference but I like them so much that I want to spell them out.

We speak the truth and face the facts.

HubSpot's people are always discussing the best approaches and everyone's input is welcome and expected, regardless of someone's position in the company. The approach in the code is, "We have the right to clear, candid, and constructive feedback. We can ask for this at any time."

The company has collected and analyzed data and the results aren't hidden; they're used for every aspect of making the company better. As the Culture Code succinctly puts it, debates are won with data, not bigger job titles. Debate and discussion can go on a long time but then someone simply has to make a decision (Just F*#king Do It). Even with all the input, every decision is not perfect but as HubSpotters say, an imperfect decision is better than no decision (ditto for a controversial decision).

We are a perpetual work in progress.

The important point of making a decision is that it becomes its own experiment. If the decision goes sideways and doesn't work out it can be revised, revisited, and the company is candid and transparent about the results and course changes. HubSpot isn't hamstrung by endless analysis. This is another example of the Anna Karenina Principle at work. Embedded in the culture is the idea that if the process doesn't work, you should fix it. Doing this gives you the chance to have a happy family.

Being a work in progress, making and reviewing decisions, and analyzing the data are more oriented toward a practice like medicine or law than to a rigid, moneymaking corporation that processes economic inputs and churns out profits. As we get away from mass markets and huge production runs, and focus on customers and subscribers, we need to be mindful that the Anna Karenina Principle will structure business models of the future.

Using good judgment is a good habit

The HubSpot Culture Code prepares people to serve the company's customers. Little of the Culture Code — beyond the data gathering and analytics — is programmed in software. Use Good Judgment is the human algorithm that everyone works by and it prepares people for all of the contingencies of life with customers that no stack of operating manuals or millions of lines of computer code could. Ultimately, the Culture Code tells employees that they are trusted to do the right thing for the customer and for the long term good of the company. Use Good Judgment is organic, heuristic, and perfect for guiding responsible people in dealing with customers' moments of truth.

It's also the perfect embodiment of Kasparov's thesis that weak people plus good technology and a solid process can make amazing things happen — more so than great technology alone. Of course, HubSpotters are anything but weak and for our purposes *average* people is a better construct.

Use Good Judgment is also the perfect complement to the Anna Karenina principle. As the principle implies, it is rare that anyone perfectly traverses the numerous potential pitfalls and glitches in any cascade. But the happy-families example is more about having ways to deal with the unexpected to address moments of truth directly and honestly, and to strive for resolution. That's what was missing in United Breaks Guitars and it's missing every time a company like Comcast tries to acquire monopoly status rather than authentically engaging with customers.

So, select for culture

Culture has to come before anything else in planning for customer relationships, as we've seen with HubSpot. Culture embodies the moments of truth you want your people to be present for. It's not enough to tell people to use good judgment; you must also point them in the right direction by letting them know what your culture stands for to the customer.

Understanding the data you need drives selection of the applications that will capture the data that drive the metrics. Metrics drive information development and ultimately produce the knowledge we all need to make good decisions. Culture is the plan of action that drives your business; it is the living embodiment of the business model.

Many companies are following HubSpot's lead or initiating their own customer-centered culture projects (see the comments on the SlideShare site where Culture Code is posted). The Culture Code reflects a younger-employee demographic, people willing to take on the challenges of working in an emerging company.

The driving customer issues that all companies face today reflect things that the youngest members of society face most squarely. In an economy that was quelled by a long and bitter recession, it's still hard to get an entry-level job and difficult to get a start in life. People are more wary of vendors with unfriendly customer policies and they are taking steps to avoid vendors that cannot or will not satisfy their needs.

Solving for the customer is rapidly crystallizing a new customer-centric ethic akin to customer experience, but less ambiguous. Solving for the customer is whole product — attention to everything that touches the customer and a good deal that stays in the back office. But importantly, it focuses on moments of truth, the things we can do something about, the things that are properly in our wheelhouses. It has little to do with customer experience strategies that ensure the buying experience is wonderful or that the user interface is pristine.

Hire vendors based on culture

Solving for the customer is not a radical idea nor does it represent a one-way street. Vendors should use good judgment when hiring people for this model and many prospective employees will certainly want to see if they can measure up to this standard. On the flip side, when these same people enter the market as customers, they also apply the new standard to their vendors.

Successful subscription companies have a built-in advantage because they solve for the customer almost without thought. Companies can't be successful with subscriptions if they aren't capturing customer data all the time and using it to drive the analytics and metrics that give them insight into what makes customers tick. This enables these companies to be in their customers' moments of truth.

SftC Takeaways

1. We've taken people out of the customer interface hoping automation could do the job at lower costs. Automation can do a lot, but sometimes it needs an assist. The trick is knowing when that is.

2. From noun to verb: turning the idea of customer experience 90 degrees.

3. Empowering employees to do the right thing for customers is the first part of the people, process, and technology fix. HubSpot wrote the book on empowering employees.

Subscription companies aren't the only ones that solve for the customer. Very large, old (and heretofore successful) companies are adopting systems and approaches to do the same. The following chapters describe approaches to building and nurturing communities, because communities generate huge amounts of customer data that drives the whole solve-for-the-customer process.

Chapter Six

Gathering Customer Data Through Community

Community is the primary data-gathering tool of Customer Science. Once we have authentic customer data we can analyze it to understand the nature of our unique moments of truth and build metrics to help evaluate our progress through Anna Karenina cascades. But what kind of community is best? There are several and each fits a narrow spectrum of needs. The next few chapters reveal their essences, how to form them, and how (and when) to use them.

Data and analysis

Community stands at the intersection of people, process, and technology because it's an efficient, cost-effective way for companies to actively engage with and listen to customers. It should replace rooms full of vendor executives trying to dictate customer policies based on old experience, hunches, focus groups, and surveys that took weeks to complete. Community is an always-on place to go to learn what customers think about products, services, policies, and procedures. It's also a place to ask open-ended questions that elicit honest responses about use, desires, and opinions on issues that might be only tangential to the business. But the findings could orient a company (under the right circumstances) toward new products and services.

ERP and CRM technologies enabled a massive paradigm shift that's not over. By the time we got around to implementing software we already were thinking differently about business and we needed the software to carry out our ambitions. Much the same is happening now during a social paradigm shift. ERP and CRM began by automating data, and ERP progressed to automating processes based on the information produced through data analysis. CRM is now at a similar point. We've automated data and realized cost savings due to efficiencies. The next level is process automation. Some may say that CRM is process automation, but if it is, why are customers so dissatisfied with our automated processes? Obviously, customer-facing processes are not as well coordinated as some vendors would like to believe.

Today's customer-facing processes — as we saw in discussing the Anna Karenina Principle — are not much more than automated transactions at a time when customers want greater precision in the actions that lead up to the transactions. Here, ERP's evolution can show the important difference.

Six Sigma, Total Quality Management (TQM), and similar approaches showed that manufacturing could be made more reliable (with significantly lower defect rates).   But it took automation of manufacturing processes — using supply chain management (SCM), ERP, and other back-office technologies — and not simply automation of manufacturing data to achieve these gains. The gains began to mount when manufacturing was able to automate process, not simply data.

So far the same thing has happened in CRM. Classic CRM automated the transactions, not the processes that directly involved customers. For example, sales force automation (SFA) automated sales people's work processes, providing a great deal of information that they had never had before. Sales reps could do office work like preparing proposals, analyzing pipelines, and more. But there was no way CRM could automate the manual, deliberative purchase process. That remains the customer's territory, much to the frustration of vendors that always want to accelerate front-office processes so that they can book revenue sooner. Automating the purchase process, of which the sales process and the transaction are only a part, requires approaches that are as novel as TQM and Six Sigma.

The customer side

The possibility of automating the customer side of the equation arrived with social media, and vendors are discovering that they need to adjust *their* business processes to align with the customer processes that have been changed by these technologies (see Chapter 3).

The revolution in social media is doing for front-office operations what ERP did for the back office. Communities represent the data gathering part of this social media revolution, and they are providing the raw material for automating customer-facing business processes. Just as ERP made improvements in industry because manufacturers could suddenly identify where processes went wrong, communities now offer companies insight into customer issues with great precision that helps them improve their customer-facing processes.

Customer moments of truth and the AKP are fundamentally about customer-process improvement. With better customer-facing processes in place, companies can justify investing in people to do the right thing for two important reasons. First, the number of things to spend time and resources on reduces to a manageable whole once moments of truth are identified. Second, a business can manage (relying on the AKP and analytics), by exception more because only the customers and the cascades that are broken or in need of intervention are teed up for attention.

A corollary of these insights is that today every company, whether it makes things or delivers services, has only one product — the way that customers experience their moments of truth— because whole product is the essential component.

Community is part of whole product because it is a bonding mechanism. Customers expect a reasonable amount of interaction with their vendors as a natural part of any product's evolution. Today's whole product includes the core product itself; the policies, procedures, and services that extend the product; and access to other users to share ideas and opinions. Companies lacking communities are failing to provide whole-product solutions that customers now expect. This failure leads to friction between vendors and customers that is detrimental to business.

Customers and Science

Vendors need to take a systematic, scientific approach to understanding customers and the social sciences are an especially good model for this type of research.[1] Not surprisingly, the social science you choose as a model will determine how successful you are. An economics-centric approach to your analysis will convince you that customers are all rational actors always making logical decisions. But it will inevitably disappoint you. If you've ever known someone who bought a car based on its color you know this.

Psychology is a popular social science especially in product marketing and it can't be ruled out for analyzing customer motivations but by its nature psychology focuses on the individual and there are simply too many individuals out there to effectively use psychology as your main social analytic tool. However, psychology is a remarkably effective tool in parts of a sales process. Ideally, though, you'll want a science that attempts to understand groups and that is sociology.

Studying customers

Studying customers is becoming a science and the scientific approach can teach business quite a lot. We often think of customers as rational actors in an economy and so we have developed numerous economic approaches to try to understand customer behavior in aggregate. Say's Law, better known as the Law of Supply and Demand is one example that uses economics, to understand the behavior of markets. But markets are not people.

Behavioral economics has emerged in recent decades as a new discipline that gets us closer to understanding how individuals might act in a marketplace. Behavioral economists use a branch of logic known as game theory when attempting to understand customer behavior, but for many things understanding customers at a behavioral level is painting the situation with a very broad brush. For one thing, assuming that is customers are rational actors is a big assumption and the adage that people do rational things for emotional reasons illustrates the point. One thing that behavioral economics gets right is the notion that behavior, at least decision-making, is based on information. The more information you have the better.

Vendors had most of the information about products and services before the rise of the Internet. You might have been able to talk to your close circle of friends about the vendor's reputation, or their experiences with the product. But you had few options other than going to the vendor if no one in your circle had experience with the vendor or product.

In many ways customers are in the driver's seat because they don't have to give up much information though they can have virtually any vendor information courtesy of the Internet, for very little investment. Also, customers have all of the information about themselves including their propensities, creditworthiness, and much more exactly what vendors crave. A customer might not regard this information as very valuable but it is. This is an unbalanced situation in which the vendors have given up control but have not yet figured out how to systematically gather customer information.

Nonetheless, customers can be studied and the findings can help vendors to do their jobs better provided they use the right lens. While understanding behavior is very good, understanding motivations for the behavior would be even better. The level of granularity is also important because we need information about how groups act at least as much as we need information about individuals.

Sociologists don't study the psychology of individuals nor do they assume that everyone is rational. Instead they study the interactions and behaviors of groups or societies taking into account how people behave in them. A customer base is one such group today because there are so many ways for individuals to share information thus forming a cohesive unit.

Sociology

The social media revolution raised an important question: Are social structures or individuals more important in shaping human behavior in the vendor-customer relationship? Before social media it might have been easy to say that social structures (specifically, the structures of the marketplace) determined how people acted because there was little choice. The relative lack of specific, independent sources of information about vendors and products created a structured market in which people had to seek out vendors to get information about things they needed or wanted. We assumed that the information was accurate but it was hard to know that until you'd bought a product.

Individual agency is the opposite of structure in this discussion. It's the ability of people to act independently to make their own free choices. The Internet and social media ushered in an age of individual agency, a time when ordinary people could empower themselves by sharing information about products and vendors free of having to interact with a vendor or consume a vendor's version of the truth. If there is a disconnect today it is because many vendors still believe they are in structured markets while most customers know they are free agents. That's the basis of today's customer lifecycle.

Dave Carroll is a free agent and so are the two million members of the failed class-action suit against Comcast. In both cases people stepped outside the prevailing structure and took ownership of their vendor-customer relationships. Neither won an outright victory but both cases irrevocably changed the marketplace, causing vendors to wake up to the new reality of customer agency.

The role of altruism

Agency's awakening got a big assist from human emotion. People are social animals. Right behind them are the herding animals that our ancestors domesticated and we inherited from antiquity. People live together and exhibit altruism and empathy, hallmarks of social behavior we're examining here.

Social animals naturally form associations and spend at least some of their time in kindred groups receiving the group's protection, accessing food, mating, and raising and protecting their young. We've seen this associative tendency in humans in earlier chapters when spontaneous groups of strangers formed on the Internet to share information that exposed vendors as enemies of the group.

Why people do this can be boiled down to altruism, that emotion that causes an individual to take a risk on behalf of a kinship group. People creating Suck Sites or contributing to sentiment sites may risk very little other than their time and perhaps a few dollars in their altruistic pursuits, but the fact that they act is still an example of altruism. The other side of altruism is trust and members of the social group tend to trust each other precisely because they have similar evidence and experiences. This is what makes social sentiment so dangerous for vendors if it turns negative. It has a ring of truth and it can go viral in an instant.

Any vendor caught in a social media meltdown will confirm that once a negative spiral starts within the customer base, it is very hard to stop. In part, it's because most vendors lack the tools to change the game.

Vendors have to adopt sociology tools and learn how to domesticate the community to solve their social media problems. Communities in the "wild" tap into the natural self-organizing tendencies we've seen. A vendor can use a domestic community to study customers if the vendor can first convince customers that its efforts are peaceful and aimed at improving the relationship they share.

The community becomes a laboratory in which the vendor, acting as sociologist, can study the behaviors and interactions of customers relative to the vendor's brand, products, and services. A lot of great information can come out of communities if they are run right.

The logical choice to run communities from the vendor side, at least for now, is the marketing group but only if at least some of the marketers can develop the specialized skills of asking open-ended questions, listening to the answers, and performing statistical analysis. By listening we mean collecting customer response data and subjecting it to analysis. Depending on the data and how it's collected, this might require a scoring mechanism that can help to turn a feeling or an opinion into numbers.

This is essentially what an NPS does, but instead of deriving a single score, a community can help a vendor first identify what's important to customers — those customer moments of truth. Once identified, a vendor should logically develop metrics and implement approaches that help to determine successful, acceptable outcomes.

Is community the new CRM?

If sociology sounds too off the radar, we can come at this point from another direction: What's the future of CRM? One answer comes from Bluewolf, a consultancy that provides implementation and development services for Salesforce.com applications. In 2012 Bluewolf launched "The State of Salesforce," an annual research report that is an interview-based survey of hundreds of Salesforce.com customers designed to surface information about customer experiences with their products and to identify emerging trends.

The 2013 edition of "The State of Salesforce" offers an important insight into CRM and where the vendor-customer relationship goes next. The research was conducted by MIT's Sloan School of Management and comprised interviews with more than 450 Salesforce.com customers to understand their perspectives on marketplace demand for front-office software — typically the province of CRM — and such applications including SFA, marketing automation, and service automation.

One of the report's more intriguing findings was that communities are the new CRM. According to the survey, 9 percent of the customers interviewed were already invested in Salesforce.com communities, while 21 percent say they were planning to subscribe to Salesforce.com communities in 2014. The surge from 9 percent to 21 percent would provide the hockey-stick graph of exponential growth we look for in accelerating markets. Given the success of other community companies like Get Satisfaction and Communispace, this would be a reasonable amount of proof, but there's a big difference between a prediction and actual results.

In an interview for *Solve for the Customer*, Bluewolf CEO Eric Berridge told me that the shift is inevitable and has already started: "For CRM to truly deliver the ROI on the billions of dollars already spent on it, it needs to cross the chasm to become more outward facing, by collecting data from every touch point a company has — especially the one between company employees and customers."

Once collected, analytics can help derive useful information that can be turned back to customers in the form or products, messages, offers, and effective processes. In fact, communities have huge benefits for vendors and customers, but vendors benefit most from having tools that enable them to deal one-on-one and in near-real time with customers.

Perhaps the biggest advantage that communities provide is in letting vendors and their managers watch social interactions among customers. Getting ideas and opinions directly from customers can be very valuable, but not as valuable as watching multiple customers discuss an idea first.

Communities can also give vendors the ability to foresee future issues and defuse negative ones. According to the Bluewolf report, the advantages of Salesforce.com communities, which are shared in many ways by other brands, include enabling "...customers, partners, product specialists, employees, suppliers, and distributers to connect and collaborate. They are also fully customizable, mobile friendly, and enable the sharing of dashboards."[2] That collaboration is what helps communities earn their keep and it's the center of a company's sociology outreach.

Communities offer the promise of enabling companies to discern moments of truth and to invest their moments of truth with actionable strategies (instead of brittle tactics). Let's examine how companies form and use communities.

Forming a Community

While communities in the wild are more or less spontaneous aggregations of people with a common interest, they're often not valuable for businesses (as we saw with the many uses of spontaneous sentiment in Chapter 2). Communities that form spontaneously do so in part prompted by altruistic impulses to warn others about a risk or danger. A business has to form the community in a way that empowers all parties to solve problems and not simply expose them if that business is going to leverage the natural participatory tendencies of a community. The community is a vessel and its members are a fluid that can occupy almost any shape; the business is responsible for forming something useful.

Mapping goals

Your goals should look a lot like the cascades of the Anna Karenina Principle as applied to your business. They are the moments of truth you want to understand better. Companies can and ought to have multiple communities that evolve over time to help them meet different marketplace challenges like product innovation, use patterns, and non-technical issues more related to the relationship than the product. The default position is to start by trying to analyze a challenge using an existing community and to only dedicate the time and resources to something that has a look of permanence. Most companies can certainly make a case for using communities to analyze issues related to products, customer-demographic types, use cases, or focus areas like sales, marketing, and service. But communities are also great places to learn about customer attitudes and unmet needs. So, it's critical to map out the goals for your first community and every time you start a new one.

Community goals should, broadly speaking, aim to show how each member could benefit from being active. Salesforce.com, Get Satisfaction, Communispace and many other vendors have developed tools and advice for customers forming communities. Some of the following ideas stem from their experiences. Here are some basic questions that can help you identify the goals for your community.

Business goals

- How can this community add to your core value proposition?

- How will this community support your company's vision, mission, and brand promise?

- How will this community complement and expand your customer experience?

- Does this community put customers at the heart of your business?

Member goals

- Who is this community for?
- What value does your product (and partnership with you) provide them?
- How can you support/serve them?
- Why should they come?
- Why would they come back?
- What motivates them to actively participate?
- Why would they participate?
- What else is competing for their attention?
- What does the sweet spot between business goals and member needs look like? Is there a lot of overlap or little?

Partner goals

Don't forget to include your partners and customers in the community and its discussions (if you work through a partner channel). Partners are an important extension of your business and working with them to maximize their impact and success will also enable them to get the most out of being associated with you. But partners are not just another form of customer; they are special, having one foot inside the tent and the other outside. So understand their needs and you'll be better able to leverage them. Ask them what their goals are.

Customer community

A successful *customer* community has to focus on relationships more than transactions. Companies already have transactional parts like sales and marketing teams, ecommerce sites, and websites. The community is different; it's your listening post, the place where you do sociology. It doesn't replace or in any way do what the transactional sites do. It's designed to build trust and relationships — the bonding that is critical to the customer lifecycle today.

Members must view the community as a safe place where they can come and ask questions without concern that their words will be misconstrued or used in any way other than how they are intended. This means there has to be a shared sense of ownership in the community that leads to improved products and services, as well as advocacy, knowledge transfer, collaboration, and value cocreation.

Partner community

A successful *partner* community has many of the same trust and collaboration drivers, but these values are expressed differently. Partners need visibility into both the value chain (to serve customers) and into product roadmaps and some business systems. It all adds up to an exchange of *information* that becomes *knowledge* for your partners. This knowledge adds value to relationships. A partner community will have a different (and probably broader) set of objectives. If you do business in both the direct and indirect channels, it might make sense to have specialist community managers for each delivery model. Below are five steps to consider — once you've mapped goals — for planning a community.

1. Budgeting and hiring a community manager

You need a budget for technology, which will probably be ongoing since most of the community solutions are offered as some form of subscription. Obviously your budget needs to include money for your manager and staff, as well as any direct costs associated with running the community. For instance, if you offer small cash awards for community activities or you give small gifts to acknowledge participation or special services to the group, you need to budget the funding. You can get a lot done in a community with just a manager (at least initially), but remember success is a happy problem.

Also, be sure to hire a real community manager (CM) and give that person a mandate. *Keep the wheels on the road* is not a mandate. This mandate is the ultimate instance of using good judgment; it's a responsibility to do what it takes to develop activities that engage customers in processes that capture customer input, analyze it for relevant information, and make it available to the whole enterprise so that people can use good judgment in serving customers with improved products, processes, policies, and services. The community manager will also work with managers and executives in sales, marketing, service, and other departments, so this person needs to be somewhat seasoned.

The community manager has to deal with numerous issues; you already know some of them, but you need to know them all — see The CM's job, below. Your project could fail if your community manager does not have a handle on all things that are tangent to a community. So even though the social realm is still new to you, this is no time for a pure on-the-job training approach.

Take legal and governance issues, for starters. Were you thinking about them? The CM has to be knowledgeable in many areas — enough to know when to get help from the legal department, for instance — and be able to take care of some issues alone. It's a real balancing act.

Also, it's easy to come up with the major community constituents like your customers, partners, and departments within the business. But what about your best customers? Should you treat them a little different? Invite them to participate in forming the community. And your company has multiple constituents to think about like the product teams, executives, marketing, support, and sales. Each constituent should be judiciously incorporated in communities when it makes sense and the CM should have the authority to compel participation — in a very nice way (as only they can do because CMs are highly social). An experienced CM has this purview and should not need to be told what to do.

The CM's job

The manager of your community is not a marketer or a sales person with a dual charter. The CM promotes productive conversations and helps to steer the community if, for instance, the conversation starts to run down a rat hole or the kids are suddenly not playing nice in the sandbox. The manager doesn't sweep things under the rug, but promotes good order by launching activities designed to foster conversation, elicit information, and encourage sharing it. There is a delicate balance to be negotiated, because the manager cannot become a gatekeeper; the manager is the facilitator of a cross-functional effort like a circus ringmaster, only better. The community manager will be the chief collector and analyzer of customer data. Think of this person as your company's sociologist doing fieldwork to understand a tribe called customers.

2. Building the community

Two kinds of construction need to happen — remember that community is very much about process. Here we'll focus on the people side of process, but later we'll look at three different community vendors and their approaches to dealing with the technology side.

Build with evolution in mind

Embrace serendipity, and let things evolve. If the growing community takes the discussion in a direction different from what you hoped for, don't fret. This is about them and the change in direction can be very informative for you. This spontaneity is what you were hoping for. Just try to ensure that you promote an atmosphere of trust and respect. It's okay to reel in the discussion if people veer off into discussing last weekend's big game but bear in mind that this is more like graduate school than first grade.

Put some early runs on the board

Start small but have goals so that you can show progress right away. Early on, any accomplishment is big because there's nothing to compare it with, but you're forming the future practices and the actual culture of the community. Start with achievable goals for your small-but-growing community and show it off to the boss — it's the boss's budget that you're spending and the higher ups always want to see progress.

3. Build community with community

This is the hard part, because of the recursive relationship between the community and building the community — through evolution it builds on itself and that takes time in early days. (It's no different from starting up a new company. How big is your first deal? It's huge, even if future deals dwarf it.) The point is that you need to get going and show some wins. An experienced manager can help with this. Your first members will have to be invited to perform the creation so selecting those first members also will be critical.

This means you will inevitably start small with a core group of members that your CM personally invited to help organize the group. From the start your focus will be to promote activity and to encourage the community to take actions independently (not waiting for your permission). Why? Because you have to be able to trust the data and information coming out of the community and you don't want to have to ask yourself if the information is reliable or if it's what the members think you want to hear. Here are some ideas for getting going.

Start small but with a big picture

Lay down some best practice ideas, such as the importance of trust and shared purpose. Ideas like these have to be acted, not simply discussed. You have to show your members the value you place on open communication and trust through joint exercises that position you as a listener. These people represent your most important stakeholders. Encourage your community members to discuss what they think is most valuable to get from the community. You may find you need to steer the discussion later to prevent it from wandering, but do it in ways that communicate you've bought into what they're telling you.

Some big ideas to get going

Community members keep coming back because they know someone is listening to what they say and because there is something new to work on, think about, and discuss. Soon enough these activities will be very focused on the business and the relationships with customers. But early activities like these five below will provide a structure to get things moving in a positive direction.

Vision statement

Community members will live by your vision statement, and they are the ones to shape it. The vision statements can answer some basic questions about why people should invest time and effort in making you (the vendor) more responsive to members' needs. Then, live up to that vision statement; there shouldn't be one thing in it that you don't actively pursue.

Create a culture of openness and trust

People have to feel welcome and respected or they won't come back (and if they do return, they might not share their ideas, which is absolutely critical). The first weeks are an important time for establishing openness and trust, and an experienced manager can be valuable here, too. Also, because this is culture and something passed on from person to person, each new recruit will go through a similar learning curve. The need for promoting trust and openness never gets old, and neither does the need to refresh the culture from time to time.

Ensure control resides in the community and not in the company

This is easy to say and hard to do. Encourage independent thought and action, and steer by asking open-ended questions. Early on, develop and promote leaders and experts in the community using badges and other recognition from gamification strategies. (As you'll see in Chapter 8 this is something that community technology company Get Satisfaction does with great success.)

Stay focused on your goals

If your community is dedicated to new-idea generation for products and services, don't turn it into a support center. Instead, build a community for peer-to-peer support. Otherwise, the people who signed up to be creative and to supply their deepest thoughts about improving your company and products may start drifting away.

Understand your limitations. If you start with a small group and each member can contribute an hour per week, you won't be effective if you put 10 big ideas in front of them and ask what they think. As the community adds more members, you can increase the number of topics. You'll then be able to get quantifiable responses even if people pick and choose what they work on.

What are the first two or three things you need to know from your community? Ask questions and generate some conclusions that you can share throughout the company. While you're at it, make sure your questioning goals and results are easily tied back to your business goals. It will both guide your next steps and build confidence in the C-suite, which is funding the community.

4. Engage with your customers on an appropriate, but intimate level

Good communities are not accidents. They're the result of planning and strategy, and you will know how well you performed the early stages leading up to this moment once the community launches. But built into every community is the idea of measurement, analysis, and applying what you know (see number 5, below). For now, get to work engaging with your customers.

CMs earn their keep through engagement. CMs have to be concerned about participation and keeping the numbers high and growing. To do this they need to frequently develop engagement programs to draw members in — it promotes constructive conversations (and maintains the community focus).

One of the CM's key functions is to encourage storytelling — a story being defined as something done with or around your company's products and services. Storytelling does two things: First, it provides the community organizer and the sponsoring company insights into customer attitudes and behaviors that they started the community to cull. People open up when they tell stories, revealing what they really think. Second, it gives others in the community content to digest and comment on, which promotes more storytelling (see number 3, on recursive activity to build communities).

Don't worry if your competition sneaks in and observes the community, too. The value of the discussion is best revealed through number crunching and sentiment analysis, which are the back-end functions of a community reserved for the sponsoring company. So, a visitor might get an idea about a topic being discussed but only the analytics will clearly show whether the percentages and trend lines are really significant.

The sad reality for many is that community participation often follows the 80/20 rule and most people are lurkers at any moment (but this shouldn't be considered a bad thing). People, quite sensibly, pick the spots most important to them when participating in issues and discussions. One individual is not likely to participate on every issue. At any time there is a core group that participates and — this is key — another group that is giving it its attention. If the silent majority didn't care they wouldn't be attentive in the first place. Keep that in mind as you think about engagement. Active listening is good.

Active listening happens in two ways: First, other community members agree with or challenge a statement and the statement can come from other members or the manager can seed them. However, the reaction is what you're looking for. Sometimes that's a story and other times it's quantitative data, it all depends on the way the manager sets up an activity. "Tell me how you feel about this..." elicits qualitative data that you can score and turn into quantitative data (if appropriate), for example. Setting up five multiple-choice questions is much more straight ahead but it might not always be appropriate and answering surveys gets old, so mix it up.

Of course, some people won't even show up (and that's a different concern), and if they aren't one reason could be that you aren't giving them anything they need from a community. That's why it's always good to ask a few "How are we doing?" questions. Stay engaged with your creation; you may be right in assuming that at some point your community can run itself but you might not like where it goes.

5. Measure, learn, adjust, repeat

Measuring results is critical but don't fall into the trap of measuring everything and then wondering what it means. You know why you are here, so refer back to your goals and make sure that you're at least measuring the things that you said at the outset really mattered to you.

Feed relevant findings back to the company and to specific people who are most interested in the results. If there are product issues they belong in the product manager's lap. Similarly, if you think you've discovered a new product or service opportunity send it to the right people in product marketing. Ditto for sales and service issues.

At many points you'll discover something you didn't know that should change the way your business operates and assuming you have the authority, you'll have to decide how to implement it. Make sure you thank the appropriate people and announce the improvement with appropriate fanfare. This doesn't mean issuing a press release as some things your community discovers go to the heart of your secret sauce. But some form of appropriate acknowledgement is needed to show your members that you are, indeed, listening.

A community is like a multiplayer online game. But there isn't just one score. Each stakeholder might have a different scoring system supported by different metrics. Customers might want problems solved or to feel validated, while executives might want to know how the community helps drive business. We don't keep score only in dollars but also with things like NPS improvements (which are surrogates for improved future business prospects). Make sure you have measurements that clearly show how well your community tracks with the goals.

Learn from what you observe. It's all part of solving for the customer: learning to make adjustments to strengthen the community then going back to it for more customer insights.

The community principles we've just reviewed work in many settings. You'll need to work through how to best implement them for your business.

SftC Takeaways

1. Understanding customer moments of truth starts with data collection and analysis. Community is the most convenient, cost effective, and touchy-feely way to get customers to tell you what they think.

2. Data capture and analysis is the beginning of Customer Science.

3. How to form communities.

Beginning in Chapter 7 we'll examine different community approaches that are appropriate for different situations. There are several ways to form and operate communities based on your objectives, how you go to market, and how your customers purchase. This helps provide the best structures for your business and customers, and ensures that agency, when used, is aimed at a productive target.

Chapter Seven

Types of Communities; The Symantec Story

Customer Science operates with customer data captured from a variety of communities. As this chapter shows, vendors can derive insights from seemingly random customer activities even when customers might not be aware that they are leaving data trails.

Community

Everything starts in community: understanding customer needs, moments of truth and relevant customer processes, and fixing problems before they become serious. Not all companies follow this prescription today, but it's a logical bet that they will.

Community combines all the human and technology attributes we've discussed to this point. It leverages individual altruism for both the member/customer and channels it for good results. Community enables the vendor to begin to demonstrate real empathy in dealing with current customer issues and in designing future scenarios that avoid problems from the start. Community is the social laboratory that companies will need to have as they enter the era when customers are subscribers — or at least think of themselves that way — and spend less time individually connecting with your representatives. It's a social laboratory that asks *why*, not just *what*.

Not every type of community fits every business's customer understanding and engagement needs. Think of the idiom *horses for courses*: Some horses run better than others in mud or in heat.

Different kinds of communities have different purposes. Horses for courses is another reason to get expert assistance before you implement a community — this new, new thing. Sure community is good, but what are you going to use yours for?

The three types of community that we'll look at here and in chapters 8 and 9 are Ad Hoc, Managed, and Mediated. Let's look at Ad Hoc from on high, then drill down.

Ad Hoc Community

Any company can (and should) have an Ad Hoc community. Some people may not call it a community, because it follows lightly the tenets of Chapter 6 regarding recruiting and building the community. Nonetheless, transparency and walking your talk are important.

Ad Hoc communities are spontaneous formations — members might not even be aware of the structure you provide. Structure, as we've seen in the connection between sociology and community, can drive organization and behavior. Ad Hoc communities still require a manager.

Your Sucks Score reveals an Ad Hoc community, that spontaneous aggregation of customers with their altruism that can give you heartburn and class-action suits. But managing an Ad Hoc community properly can avert that and help you build trust and respect, not anger and lawsuits.

Managed Community

A Managed Community is the workhorse of the community spectrum and requires relatively more resources from your business. The community is run like another (small) department. Depending on its size a company with a managed-community approach probably has multiple communities going on at once (and possibly multiple kinds of communities), supporting individual product lines, brands, departments, and other important sectors of the business.

Running a Managed Community is not a solo process. As we'll see in Chapter 8's Hewlett Packard use case, which uses customer-engagement platform Get Satisfaction, there's plenty of participation and coaching from Get Satisfaction. But HP Vertica is in control and does all the work.

Mediated Community

A Mediated Community is different from a Managed Community in several key respects. Most notably, your community manager runs the managed kind while a services provider mediates a community doing most of the work and reports to your community manager regularly. There are good reasons for each.

A Mediated Community's goals are often slightly different from those of other communities. Companies like Communispace are in the business of helping their customers to discover things about their end customers that go into new product development and process design, among other things. Communispace's customer list includes Charles Schwab, Hallmark, and Nabisco, plus many others that want to understand their customers' needs at a detailed level. Communispace has a rich diversity of people on staff with interdisciplinary skills in technology as well as in social sciences.

Another difference found in the Mediated Community, Communispace style, is that it's relatively temporary and small — unlike a Managed Community that may take on all comers and have tens of thousands of members. In many ways the Mediated Community is the closest to sociology fieldwork.

Communispace recruits a few hundred community members with specific backgrounds that their clients want to know something about. Communispace communities may only last for a few months, long enough to satisfy the objectives of the research brief.

In many engagements, Communispace may serially empanel multiple communities. There are good reasons for this approach. For instance, community members are often selected for their seniority and positions as decision makers. They lead busy lives and can't dedicate an indefinite amount of time to community membership, but many are happy to lend a hand for a time.

Both managed and mediated approaches give community vendors the ability to stay in their customers' businesses as strategic partners, providing value added services that make their products more effective and impactful for the end customers and more profitable for the vendor. A company like Get Satisfaction treats its customer base like another community showing that they walk their talk and, importantly, this approach to service provides the company with an additional revenue source.

Let's turn our attention to the Ad Hoc community model and the specific instance of one sponsored by Symantec.

Ad Hoc Communities — Knowing Your Jetsam and Flotsam

An Ad Hoc Community forms whenever people converge on an issue though they may not be aware of each other. Your company and its products can easily be the convergence points (and Suck Sites maybe the original example). Ad Hoc Communities instituted by vendors take the initiative: Rather than simply being a place to complain, these sites leverage social media to understand and react to the market. But getting from a lot of tweets to getting a knowledge set that you can derive business benefit from is part art and part science.

All the social media and website data, plus the random input you collect, create a pile of data that is potentially valuable to your company, but only if you have a way to sort through it to find the nuggets of information you need to run your business. When you have the information, you're no longer blind to the realities of your customers. Next up is turning the information into knowledge by identifying the things to address in the short, intermediate, and long terms. This starts with sorting and scoring.

The key to sorting is granularity. Each sorted group should kick off a business process with people behind it to resolve issues or otherwise process the data. Many sorts result in many processes, so it's important to establish groupings that make business sense but that do not impose too much business overhead. Every issue can't be unique — in my experience, seven or eight sorts (buckets) is a good number. The sorts should reflect what your customers say are their moments of truth (always keep the Anna Karenina Principle in mind).

There are multiple kinds of knowledge you might want to collect about your customers that fit the AKP well. Below, a list of seven buckets to consider — you can add to these buckets for your unique business.

1. **Help!** Any Ad Hoc Community initiative worth its salt should recognize a customer cry for help. It can include questions about billing, product use, or delivery issues for starters. But typically we distinguish a help request as something that needs a product specialist's attention. (Compare this with an Inquiry, number 3, below.)

2. **Sales lead**. You simply have to know when a customer is teeing you up and waiting for your swing. They don't wait forever and you shouldn't think that every inquiry is a sales opportunity, either. Teaching hospitals coach new doctors to distinguish between relatively rare zebras and more common horses when diagnosing a malady (when you hear hoof beats think horses not zebras). They get points for being right, not for being exotic. You can apply this idea to your business, too. Don't try to force things into the sales category but frequently when a customer describes an issue that can only be solved with your new product you have to be able to process the need efficiently. So give this a bucket of its own.

3. **Inquiry.** This is a question that doesn't require the attention of the rocket scientists who invented your product or even the finance group. Customer service people, FAQ systems, and other customers can answer many inquiries — many customers are happy to help if given the chance. Have you enlisted your customers to helping each other?

4. **Tirade, rage, bluster, rant, fume, seethe, harangue, suck!** Angry customers are still customers, so be happy you uncovered this sentiment: At least the customer is still talking to you. The good news is that you know about it and so have a chance to turn the situation around before another Sucks Site entry is added to the Internet. This is what the Anna Karenina Principle is all about — finding a broken moment of truth — and it's your chance to make a lasting impression, so make it a good one.

5. **Rave, kudos, endorsement.** Oh, happy day! You can't get enough of these. Most often these are the result of someone on your team going above and beyond (and using good judgment) for the good of the enterprise. And while you ought to be able to identify these instances and, to the extent possible, take a victory lap, don't forget the person on your team who made it possible. Remember HubSpot's Culture Code (Chapter 5) — share credit, shoulder responsibility.

6. **Feature request.** You get these all the time; a single request isn't enough to change your product plan, but you do need to capture and catalog it for stack-ranking purposes and refer to the list from time to time. New products get started this way and it's R&D on the cheap. But be aware that a new feature request can also be a masked form of another kind of feedback that you can turn into knowledge. For example, a customer who doesn't know enough about how to use your product might ask for a feature when what the customer really needs is training in the existing functionality. Another customer may even resolve this kind of inquiry or it may be a sales opportunity.

7. **Fraud.** There are all kinds of jetsam and flotsam on the Internet. Filtering the stream for a product name may occasionally reveal someone doing something they shouldn't with your brand, logo, or product. You should know about it and take action.

So, back to Anna Karenina. You're never going to have all the BARs line up on the slot machine of business. Something that can go wrong will but if you understand that filtering the Internet stream for customer sentiment can reveal valuable knowledge that you can use to make your business better and to better serve your customers, why wouldn't you? It's as simple as these three steps:

1. Understand these seven buckets (or however many your business needs).

2. Fill them and then analyze the contents.

3. Develop procedures and processes that make all the steps second nature.

Filtering, scoring, and bucket process flow

Filtering is a crude form of scoring. Once an issue is scored workflow rules should deposit the issue in the right business process for resolution. There may even be other processing steps to consider. For instance, if a customer has a service level agreement (SLA) with you, anything that requires a response should be stack ranked, flagged, and timed so that you'll meet the SLA. Think of the SLA as a formalized moment of truth with the possibility of a penalty. Actually, you may want to consider imposing your own SLAs on different buckets. For example, a problem report should have a faster turn around than an enhancement request.

Each bucket should have its own process flow — some things are critical and some not. Managing this is one of the easiest things you can do to save resources without diminishing the quality of your relationships.

If you're a customer on the other hand...

Have you been a good customer? I'm not talking about how much stuff you've bought — that just makes you a consumer. But as a customer you should know that you have an important responsibility in the various ecosystems you've bought into called engagement. Engagement doesn't only happen when you have a complaint (it shouldn't feel like a full time job, either).

You won't participate in every ecosystem you buy from all the time — you don't have the time or resources — so pick your spots using the voice you naturally have within the ecosystem. It means not simply making a purchase or stalking off if someone does something you don't like or adding one more Sucks Site to the Internet that no one, even vendors, pays attention to. (True, search engines do pay attention to them, but they're robots.)

But sometimes vendors don't listen. Make yourself heard in an adult way by providing accurate and responsible feedback to your vendors. Now that you have a better idea of how you as a vendor can accumulate, sort, and respond to your input, you have almost everything you need to get better outcomes. I am not saying this will be easy; many vendors don't have the customer orientation religion yet. But you can help there, too.

The customer experience

Much of this chapter is about the customer experience, an overused phrase. Many people simply mean the literal experience that customers have using your product or service. Was the bed too firm, too soft, or just right? You get the idea.

The customer experience is what you engineer for the customer, just as much as you engineer the product, packaging, and training. A customer experience isn't only the backward look at what happened in the course of an everyday interaction. Customers now have so much ability to rate and rank, to influence others, and to affect your bottom line that you don't have time to wait until someone has a problem they want settled before you think about the customer experience. Instead, you should be designing every encounter (moment of truth) that a customer has with your company — on the web, through social media, in a store, at a conference, or in a trade show booth. That design has to take into account what you know about your customers from the data you've collected and analyzed, and how you want to steer the conversation.

The Symantec Story

Symantec is the largest supplier of security software in the world. It developed a community strategy using the Sales Cloud and Radian6 from Salesforce.com that incorporates many of the concepts for Ad Hoc Communities noted above. The plan is showing good results, according to company representatives, though they're not ready to make any hard-number pronouncements. Symantec was happy to share its ideas for *Solve for the Customer*.

As you might expect with a new idea like social CRM and employing it in customer service, when Symantec got started there were various products on the market and lots of vendor claims. But what seemed to be lacking was a consolidated, end-to-end process or set of procedures that could turn a lot of software, good intentions, and theories into practical, usable business knowledge that would also yield tangible results.

Symantec started its community work by asking a series of simple questions: What do we want to get back from this effort? To know when someone says something about Symantec? To know what they say? It turned out that the company simply needed to know what was being said that was actionable. Virtually every company gets mentioned on the Internet and in social media, but only a portion of the mentions needs to be acted on. Some mentions may be anonymous (thus not able to be followed up); others may be innocuous and a follow-up might seem Big Brotherish. Still other mentions may be simply in bad taste or in jest, neither of which is necessarily actionable. So the Symantec team came up with an idea and a term that ideally described what it was looking for: Actionable Internet Mentions™ (AIMs), and the company trademarked it. Actionable Internet Mentions means:

1. A mention that requires analysis or engagement according to Symantec's sorting rules (i.e., AIMs represent a customer moment of truth.

2. AIMs have to be posted on publicly visible social media.

3. Someone who is not employed by Symantec must post AIMs.

Symantec developed a strategic sorting of its social stream in search of things it could do something about, largely ignoring what was out of this scope. To become AIMs, social-stream items need to pass through several filters.

The next step was to build a classification system that enabled Symantec to sort AIM into buckets that would best use the talents of specialist employees. These classifications need to be identified before they can all be consolidated into the AIMs definition. It's a small point, but one that the Symantec team deserves credit for figuring out.

AIMs are actionable because Symantec knows who the customer making a declaration is, and because an issue is a moment of truth fitting into an Anna Karenina cascade that the company always wants to do something about when it has the chance, especially because it's public. By addressing public sentiments as moments of truth with speed and precision, Symantec prevents the start of a negativity chain and produces better, more relevant customer experiences.

This approach won't enable you to address every malcontent. It only surfaces the people and issues that get some play in social media. There are people who really would walk into McDonald's and ask to weigh a quarter pounder, and there's not a lot to do about it. But those people are few and far between, and their credibility suffers as a result of their rants. For the same reasons *you* find it difficult to communicate with them, other people tend to distrust them because they display ego, not altruism. So focus on doing the greatest good for the greatest number.

The classifications that the Symantec team came up with made sense for that company and the job it was trying to do. Your classification scheme might look a little different. Here's the list (not in order of importance):

1. Case: A request for help resolving a real-time issue.

2. Query: A question that doesn't require a support resource.

3. Rant: An insult that merits brand-management consideration.

4. Rave: Praise from a Symantec brand advocate.

5. Lead: An announcement of a near-term purchase decision.

6. RFE: A request for enhancement.

7. Fraud: Some form of communication from someone unauthorized to sell Symantec products.

Most of these items look like common sense to a trained eye in customer support. What's remarkable about it is that first, it all can be done through automation and, second, that it can be pulled from the Internet, an atypical (or non-traditional) source of customer feedback. Last, it's also very reliable for finding fraud. Although it's hard to pinpoint how much revenue a company like Symantec might recover from this kind of fraud detection, prior to the AIMs approach, the company had a much harder time identifying it at all.

This triage process is straightforward. Symantec uses Radian6 from Salesforce.com, part of its Marketing Cloud, to capture the social stream and sort it by product and then according to the classification rules Symantec had set up. Symantec sorts by product first because the company has many and this helps streamline product specialists' review process. When the stream gets to the seven-classifications filter, it is split and individual cases quickly get routed to specialist employees charged with dealing with them. Symantec employees then provide appropriate responses to customers through the same social media channel that originally brought in the AIMs.

This first initiates a conversation between the company and its customer and the approach has a high hit rate because the process can happen fast enough to send a reply while the customer is still in the social medium. Second, it happens as a "good" surprise for many people. Imagine what it's like to be complaining about something and to receive a completely unexpected response nearly right away — that's something that a sentiment site can't do. Third, many times an issue can be put to bed with one interaction, especially if the employee is also sending links to helpful information from a knowledgebase or a video archive.

The result is remarkable. Forget for a moment all the good things that can happen when a company thanks a customer for a compliment. When a customer is in a negative mindset, receiving a cheerful and near instantaneous response with help or a solution can prevent the negativity from hardening, can even turn a negative into a positive, possibly helping to bond the complainer (turning that person into an advocate).

This is what makes customer bonds and it's a good example of the Anna Karenina Principle in action. Happy families are happy because they work through their difficulties with respect and transparency, not because they're perfect.

Results so far

Symantec says its results are encouraging. The approach generates a great deal of data from which the company can extract useful information like classification of issues by product line. Any company with multiple products will have some that are relatively trouble-free and others that are more support intensive. This kind of insight can be valuable.

The point of extracting product-specific information isn't to assign blame to anyone or on any product, but to make comparisons over time that enable vendors to drive improvement. Symantec has the ability with this approach to compare product lines year over year (or more frequently). It also has the ability to compare a classification pattern by customer type, such as enterprise versus consumer. Is fraud a bigger issue in the enterprise or on the consumer side? Symantec doesn't have to guess at that answer — it has hard information, which enables better business decisions.

The upshot

A pattern begins to emerge from all this. We can use the Internet and applications available there, combined with in-house tools, to craft a new approach to managing customer relationships. Generally, it involves these three components:

1. **Collecting customer data**. The more diversity in your data collection the better. Don't worry about the amount or the type of data (most of it will be useless — you have to sift through gravel to find gold).

2. **Sorting and scoring.** Good algorithms will do the hard work of separating the gold, which will set you up nicely for the refining process, a.k.a. analysis.

3. **Analyzing.** You've collected a lot of gold nuggets, but you aren't finished. You need to refine the gold and pour it into molds to make bars. At that point you have information and knowledge about customers that you can use to make smart decisions about what to do next. Maybe that means responding with a solution, but it can also mean making an offer that fits a need, sending an enhancement request to the product team, or chasing down some fraudulent use of your product or brand.

SftC Takeaways

1. Three types of community, each has a purpose.

2. You can learn a lot from just filtering the Internet.

3. Symantec's success with an Ad Hoc Community.

We can take the same basic techniques to a more proactive (and semiprivate) environment, where customers meet and discuss various aspects of a company and its products in Managed and Mediated Communities. It also takes a bit more work, as chapters 8 and 9 will reveal.

Chapter Eight

A Managed Community: HP Software's Big Data Business Unit and Get Satisfaction

The workhorse community of Customer Science is the Managed Community and in this chapter we look at how HP Software's Big Data business unit leveraged a Managed Community from Get Satisfaction to engage customers.

Greater range with a Managed Community

Symantec's strategic filtering of the social stream has been able to collect valuable customer data to support multiple in-house business processes. This Ad Hoc–community approach is a good fit for the need, but it only goes so far. Specifically, filtering the stream gives you what's top of mind for people on social media at a moment in time. What about those times when customers think about something but don't share it? A customer may have a great idea or that person might be simmering in unhappiness about something of which the vendor is completely unaware.

You need to ask customers what they think if you really want to know more about them. This was quite hard to do until the social-media revolution. The number of customers you could touch through a survey or focus group was relatively small and yielded qualitative results. Now there are two types of community that support the vital business process of listening. This chapter looks at Managed Communities, which are exemplified by the HP experience with Get Satisfaction.

A Managed Community has several differences compared to Ad Hoc communities (see Table 8.1 below). It can help you elevate your game because rather than waiting for a problem to surface in an Ad Hoc community, you can be proactive and this beats filtering random posts from the stream in many situations. That's why a Managed Community is a better bet, in some cases, than the Ad Hoc variety. Of course, Ad Hoc Communities have their uses. Horses for courses, remember: Use the right tool for your situation.

In a Managed Community the community manager acts on behalf of the business to conduct research designed to bring in useful customer data that is analyzed to uncover customer issues and needs in depth. The process can turn ideas into gold for your company. Unlike an Ad Hoc Community, a Managed Community is administered daily with the intent of uncovering something new, not gathering over-the-transom material.

Ad Hoc	Managed
Handled within the business.	Vendor and customer meet on more neutral ground.
Episodic, one and done.	Interactive and iterative.
Data focused; simple processes.	Process focused; data that's generated is analyzed offline for later use in a variety of ways.
Primarily tactical, though it can be used to uncover new concepts. Not designed for open-ended questions or direct many-to-many dialogue. Dialogue is one-to-many, with no expectation of reply. May be constrained by Twitter's 140-character limit.	Tactical and strategic. The ability to ask open-ended questions of the community and let the answers come in asymmetrically enables deeper thought by customers and a chance to trade ideas and to mature a concept under discussion. The vendor also has greater ability to observe customer-to-customer interactions than with an Ad

	Hoc Community.

Table 8.1 Differences Between Ad Hoc and Managed Communities

Managed Communities tend to straddle stovepipes. They're partly about service and support, partly about gathering new ideas, and always about helping to develop bonds between members and between members and the brand or company sponsoring the community.

A Managed Community may also focus on a common issue, rather than a product or brand. These communities are more about spreading thought leadership — they can be very effective. Thought-leadership communities usually have obvious sponsorship and content is used for support and inbound marketing, something that HubSpot, for example, specializes in (see Chapter 5).

There are two kinds of information a company can reap from a Managed Community: direct feedback from customers, which comes from surveying the members and asking open-ended questions; and indirect feedback, which is generated when a group discusses an issue. The community manager tees up many questions but members contribute questions, too: What does the group think? How does this change over time? Are some members able to convince others of an alternative viewpoint? Who are they demographically and what do their ideas mean to the company and its products? What is the result of the discussion?

Ad Hoc and Managed communities are great venues where new customers, or those considering a first purchase, can go to learn from experienced users about the benefits and shortcomings of products and vendors. This is one place where bonding meets reality and can become advocacy.

Newbies can also get a great deal of practical advice about first use and, with ongoing participation, solving problems. There's nothing like hearing from someone who had your problem and figured out a solution. It's great for the new customer and great for the helper. It's also great for the vendor if a problem can be resolved to everyone's satisfaction without the vendor's people and resources being expended.

Ad Hoc communities primarily manage customer social data. A big part of managing these communities involves applying processes — sorting and segmenting into different buckets with SLAs attached to them. But because the customer doesn't perceive a process or necessarily interact with a company's people, the approach is more a random data-management process than it is a customer-centered process. After all, the fundamental process is to generate a trouble ticket or other action item for something that comes into a company through social media, not necessarily to engage with the customer. This resembles a conventional CRM process much more than it resembles a social encounter.

The HP Vertica Story

Hewlett-Packard's formerly independent Vertica business unit — which as of November 2014 is now part of the big data business unit of HP Software — provides an interesting use story about community and many of the forces driving modern business. The business sits at the intersection of subscriptions, technology, big data, and community.

The HP Vertica Analytic Platform is a technical product aimed at technical users. It's a purpose-built analytics platform that enables companies to monetize their data at a scale and speed demanded by business. HP Vertica delivers considerable value to customers by providing analytics and data warehousing that's useable immediately, unlike older technologies that typically require a long development cycle.

Vertica's business model overlaps several different models, unlike many analytics vendors who sell licenses or apply a subscription model to their businesses. HP makes Vertica available as a free download (the Vertica Community Edition), to any customer that wants to use it. Numerous organizations download and test Vertica for their analytics needs each week; there are thousands of customers worldwide already using the product. The use can be on in-house servers or those provided by infrastructure-subscription vendors, including HP's Helion unit and third-party providers. Either way, any company managing up to a terabyte of data will pay no license fees to HP.

This freemium model, as it's known in the business, carries with it some interesting challenges. Primarily, customers usually need some technical expertise and coaching to get up to speed. But without a revenue stream it's hard to justify support personnel, so HP's strategy has been to use the freemium model in part as a marketing device to engage technical buyers. At some point these buyers prove the concept within their companies and some become paying customers as their deployments exceed the 1 TB–limit of the freemium.

In addition to the goodwill support provided by HP engineers and others in the community, much of the support that users receive comes from other sources, such as other customers and third-party vendors, who've developed products and services that help round out the core Vertica offering. HP's example has also filtered down to the partners who are members of a solutions marketplace or ecosystem. Their models also leverage the freemium approach.

Chris Selland

The Managed Community approach was an inspiration of Chris Selland, who at the time was VP of marketing for HP Vertica, and now runs business development and strategic alliances for the big data business unit of HP Software. Selland's 20 years of experience in the industry exposed him to many emerging ideas, models, and vendors, and when he got to HP Vertica he knew immediately that to expand the rapidly growing community of Vertica users and to support the freemium model, HP Vertica would have to develop a Managed Community that would provide a channel for peer-to-peer support and expose HP Vertica to more customer ideas for documentation and product improvement. He hoped that a Managed Community would also shoulder some of the support needs for Vertica's Community Edition, and foster constructive interaction with the growing partner community.

HP Vertica chose Get Satisfaction, a San Francisco–based company offering community technology as a subscription service, for the Managed Community. Get Satisfaction provides community software and the services needed to optimize any implementation.

HP Vertica's community goals

HP Vertica gave me direct access to its community-oriented staff and permitted me to interview Get Satisfaction's customer success manager for *Solve for the Customer*. All quotes below are from that research.

Part of assessing a company's readiness for adopting a community involves developing and understanding its goals. For instance, communities can be dedicated to better marketing, selling, or supporting customers but some may be product centric, HP Vertica wanted to be able to listen better to those customers, who in the end can affect all of these areas.

HP Vertica had previously offered a customer forum that required registration and a sign in before the community project started. Its most helpful customer-focused information was buried deep in the forum. Consequently, it was hard to find and not often accessed. It was not unusual to see the same customer questions asked repeatedly, which required more work for the staff and indirectly fostered the development of an independent forum that was more accessible by users. But that forum, while useful, didn't have all the rich information content that HP Vertica held, and wasn't easily searchable or accessible. It left customers with the unenviable choice of either a community without sufficient information or a hard-to-access information vault.

The team

HP Vertica's small team included Jason Bailey, senior manager of digital marketing, and Danielle Sandahl, global campaigns manager. Not only was it good business, it also fit well with a strategy that aimed to attract new customers through a try-and-perhaps-buy model. To accomplish this goal HP Vertica had to bring together multiple departments affected by the community and had to convince some people of a direction change involving greater transparency using information of all kinds.

The project involved in-house groups. The documentation team wanted to better understand if there were gaps in its documentation and other content offerings. Support needed to see if it could deflect some calls to other parties, thus helping balance its workload while still offering great service. This was important since some customers were on the freemium edition and every service encounter represented a cost. Last, Sandahl says, "In marketing we wanted search engine optimization and to have everything out in the open so that we could get more people interested in Vertica."

HP Vertica was well aware that some of its customers were already self-organizing into constructive communities for mutual support. Third-party developers were creating their own workarounds and plug-ins, and they needed a place where they could engage and trade ideas, which gave rise to these independent forums.

The forums were good for organizing and promoting engagement among HP Vertica customers, but because those communities were outside of the business, the company had little ability to see into them to capture data for analysis and generally engage in community activities from a vendor perspective. So, even at the beginning of the official HP Vertica community, the team knew it would have to incorporate the outside groups and the sharing they represented if the community was going to be successful.

Not everyone thought incorporating the outside groups into the community was a good idea at this stage, and there was a good deal of skepticism about the value of other groups, especially since the HP team couldn't see into these forums the way it would eventually see into its own community. But as Sandahl says, it was a good early lesson in transparency. "The goal was to be the most helpful person in the room when someone's trying and get an answer." So the forum was no hindrance in that effort, "When we took a step back," she says, "we realized that this was fantastic. We have people that are so passionate about our product that they're willing to start their own forums to talk about it and collaborate on it."

Very quickly the forum and the community emerged with their own styles and followings, which also overlapped. Despite the fact that HP Vertica was not first to form a community, it was able to recruit customers simply by reaching out to them. I interviewed Lori Jenkins, former customer success manager of the community vendor Get Satisfaction, for *Solve for the Customer*. Jenkins, who worked with the HP Vertica team during the rollout, says, "They simply reached out to all those people and said to them, 'We love what you're doing. We've created a place for you to do it, come join us. And they did.'"

The forum and community provided complementary experiences for users, and remain places where advocates can meet and provide peer support. HP Vertica engineers are also available at the community to take inquiries, and as Sandahl says, it serves as a professional forum. "We're not the type to lock our engineers in the back room and not let them talk to people. We're more than happy for them to talk about the product that they're so proud of and make sure that everyone that's using it sees success in doing so."

Enter Get Satisfaction

One of the things that immediately distinguish SaaS companies like Get Satisfaction from more conventional businesses is the amount of service typically available from the vendor. Subscription vendors need to ensure that all customers engage and succeed with their products, because it's so easy for customers to change their minds, resulting in churn or attrition, and lost revenue. Successful SaaS companies take a hands-on approach to customers.

SaaS systems enable vendors to track customer use as a customer success marker. When metrics indicate a problem, many SaaS companies deploy customer-success managers (CSMs) to evaluate and fix problems. But nothing is better than avoiding any startup problems before they begin, so Get Satisfaction offers a range of training- and implementation-assistance programs (some of which are separately charged for) to get customers off on the right foot. HP Vertica took advantage of Get Satisfaction's implementation assistance to get its community off the ground.

Mentoring

Get Satisfaction assigns a launch director to help customers correctly deploy their technology. It also uses a customer-success manager (CSM). As the title implies, the CSM's mission is to make the customer succeed with the product, an effort that's part of a strong movement in support of customer success that many subscription businesses are taking on. For HP Vertica, this assignment went to Jenkins, who has a unique skill set. She is a former elementary school teacher, knows how to organize people, and how to craft an implementation plan to initiate customer-participation activities that help identify moments of truth, resulting in optimal use of her product. Most important, she knows how to listen.

Think of Jenkins or any CSM as a process coach, a person who can help a novice business to build and begin operating a community and its processes by designing the vehicle and initiating some customer-participation activities that help identify some moments of truth.

Importance of trust

Promoting a trusting environment where people can feel free and are encouraged to reveal their thoughts without fear of criticism is a challenging, subtle process. Trust doesn't happen through an edict, a command, or a policy dictated at the top. It has to be earned through implementation and community leadership has to first take actions that walk the talk.

Get Satisfaction has compiled a Customer Company Pact that illustrates how to build a trusting, productive community environment (see Table 8.2). The pact's points make a short, practical primer for participating in a community from either side of the vendor-customer line.

For Customers	For Companies
Be Understanding — **Show the respect and kindness to people inside the company that you'd like shown to you.**	Be Human — **Use a respectful, conversational voice, avoid scripts and never use corporate doublespeak.**
Be Yourself — **Use a consistent identity and foster a long-term reputation with the company.**	Be Personal — **Encourage staff to use their real names and use a personal touch.**
Be Helpful — **Recognize that problems will occur and give companies the information and time required to competently address issues.**	Be Accountable — **Make it easy to contact you and cultivate a public dialogue with customers to demonstrate your accountability.**
Be Fair — **Share issues directly, or in a community where the company has an opportunity to respond, so it can work with you to solve problems.**	Be Ready — **Anticipate that problems will occur and set clear, public expectations in advance for how you will address (and redress) issues.**
Be Open — **Give companies the benefit of the doubt and be open to what they have to say.**	Be Earnest — **Demonstrate your good intentions by speaking plainly, earnestly and candidly with customers about problems that arise.**

Table 8.2 The Get Satisfaction Customer Company Pact

In HP Vertica's case it's important to understand that community is a unique channel. Jenkins says, "We often have support people manning this channel. But they have to remember that this isn't about generating a trouble a ticket, though that's one possible outcome. In a community, you're not an anonymous agent." The more human presence you bring to your community, the better you show that you're walking your talk.

Here the Get Satisfaction application was instrumental to helping convey a sense of humanness. For instance, Jenkins says: "I always tell people not to use their company logo instead of their personal photo. But I also recommend that they only use their first names and that they include their job titles. I think getting away from the anonymous, and the corporate is really what you need to build trust."

Readiness assessment

Jenkins's first job in any new deployment is to figure out where the new customer is on an implementation readiness spectrum. This includes evaluating a company's culture, its people, and the goals of the community, and sets a course of action designed to get everyone on the same page. Get Satisfaction has accumulated its own list of key success factors that it uses to benchmark a new customer from many perspectives, such as a company's culture and its technology environment.

After her analysis, and with an accurate sense of what needs to be accomplished in the community, Jenkins designs a mentoring project. Typically, she meets early on once or twice a week in workshop sessions designed to keep the rollout on track, make suggestions, and evaluate status. As Jenkins says, "These sessions go from high level all the way down into the weeds. So we get into all the key tactics for implementing and running a community."

Jenkins worked primarily with HP Vertica's Sandahl, who is responsible for the marketing and communications, email communications, and most third-party advertising, the community, and lead generation.

Company culture

Communities can prosper within a variety of company cultures. Some will be better than others for a given community type, and establishing and running a community will inevitably begin to modify a company's culture. The whole organization will trend toward becoming more reflective of the transparent, sharing, open entity that a community needs to be. A healthy community reflects a healthy culture; a healthy culture sponsors a healthy community.

As an example of a company culture from an earlier implementation that needed work, Jenkins described a situation where management bought into a community but failed to notify the product team. "That's a big problem," she says.

Perhaps the only kind of company culture incompatible with community is one that is undocumented, chaotic, and lacks self-awareness. HubSpot's story (see Chapter 5) is a good example of a company culture that is naturally set up for community: It's well documented, organized through self-awareness, enabling, and transparent. It empowers people to do the right things by supporting decision-making and is self-aware and ready to analyze inputs and outputs in an effort to get even better.

Fortunately, HP Vertica had a really good culture already in place. Jenkins says: "I walked out of my first meeting with HP Vertica with a huge smile on my face because I thought that as a culture and as a company, they were ready take on a community. They did something unique that not everyone does — they brought everyone in on the mentoring calls."

HP Vertica invested its people's time in the community rollout thereby empowering them. In addition to the teams from support, product development, and marketing, teams from technical content and documentation, as well as the Salesforce.com administrator, were included because the community would feed data into the CRM system as well as access it. Jenkins recalls that they got off on the right foot. "Right off the bat they said, 'Hey, we all each have our own processes. Now we need to bridge them for this community,'" she says.

So HP Vertica brought its people together, which demonstrated the importance of the project and the company's support for it. As the meetings progressed, Jenkins says, "I'd ask a probing question to see what they thought about a particular tactic. Everyone would answer something different, and in some company cultures, that would be a problem. Things might get awkward or they would find it a problem. These guys would just start to laugh and say, 'Oh, well, I guess it's good that we're talking about it.'"

Jenkins says that other phrases frequently heard in the mentoring meetings include, *Oh, that's so good that we surfaced that. Why do you think that it should work this way? How about you? What do you think?*

No one at HP Vertica saw any of the community building experience as a negative. "They were totally willing to just face all of that with humor and openness," Jenkins says. All points of view and all existing processes were treated with understanding and respect, which helped to cement the kind of trusting environment that would become invaluable when customers were brought into the mix.

Nevertheless, the process did have some growing pains, according to Sandahl. "One of our first steps was to pull our documentation out from behind the wall, and ensure that people could get to it. And for some, that was a really big deal, because [to them] it felt like we were handing over the cookbook to our competitors." But it made sense, too, because the company wanted to reach out to its freemium users and to provide enhanced support options to its paying customers. That's when the idea of being the most helpful person in the room, in Sandahl's words, became a reality.

Jenkins summarizes the culture she walked into at HP Vertica this way: "They showed a real willingness to work across departments and complete motivation to face all of that with humor and openness. I thought that was amazing."

Handling negativity

Part of the being-human advice means being brave enough to take risks with how others will perceive you. It's easy to let things become a little negative in the Internet's impersonal world, which adversely impacts trust issues and can retard sharing, the ultimate goal of any community. That's one reason for the Customer Company Pact. Of course, pacts have their limits and need reinforcement with actions — walking the talk.

Jenkins explains: "One time we had a new intern who accidentally sent out a marketing campaign twice to the same person by accident. The customer complained in our community, and said, 'I don't even know if she's a real person.' To diffuse the situation we had the intern write back and say, 'Hi. It was me. I'm so sorry. I made a mistake.' It's things like that — just being human — that really help keep everything positive."

Sometimes, managing a community might require more discipline. Sandahl relates a story about a customer who had been contributing positively to the community for many months, but whose contributions became increasingly negative even while this person became more active. "I didn't want to block his access because he had been contributing in a very, very helpful manner for a very long time," she says. "But it was surprising to see this kind of backlash coming from him. So I reached out to Lori and asked how we should handle this?"

For the good of the community they decided to gently confront the person on an individual basis. "We said, 'We want to know exactly what you think of the product and the community, and if there's any way for us to fix something, we'd be more than happy to work with you as a champion in our community to move forward with anything that you might suggest to help improve it.'" That was all it took. After the person took a break from the community, he resumed making positive contributions and the crisis passed. But Sandahl also says: "We have a special eye on him to make sure that it doesn't get negative again. I think us reaching out to him at least set the tone for the relationship that we want to have with him going forward."

Adding metrics

Community interactions are in many cases completely opposite to the way human communication has evolved: face-to-face and in the moment. We take for granted human nature's ability to read non-verbal cues when two people interact, but when those cues are removed it can illuminate how valuable they are. Without the non-verbal cues that are naturally built into direct communication, businesses have to adjust by capturing and analyzing other data to fill the void. Metrics are critical in operating any community, primarily because interactions are digital, somewhat impersonal, and asynchronous. Metrics help fill in the details — the body language — that indirect communication can remove from an interaction.

Bailey was primarily responsible for metrics and HP Vertica had multiple data sources and the respective analytics to choose from, including the community, the partner marketplace, the live-user version of Vertica, Vertica.com, Salesforce.com, and popular social sites.

Get Satisfaction comes with built-in analytics (from its partner GoodData) that provide metrics on community data. The community site quickly enables users to define metrics using GoodData but metrics are also delivered with a complement of 10 tabs full of prebuilt analytics. Get Satisfaction calls its product Community Health Analytics because it focuses on metrics that help users to understand uptake and use characteristics. It's also a concrete example of how to walk your talk.

But as a technology company and as an analytics vendor, HP Vertica is also interested in the broader use of analytics. Bailey developed a dashboard in HP Vertica that brings together data from all his data sources.

Some of the metrics Bailey and others use to gauge the success of the community include page views of documentation, the number of different topics raised, the number of direct views of comments, and the number of new users. Ideally, all should be increasing and that's what Bailey sees these days. Referring to one of the community's original goals of making information accessible to customers, in a recent month there were 20,000 views of comments representing customers asking and answering questions, and deriving value from the interaction. Bailey says, "This represents successful deflection, because people get their questions answered, and often it's without assistance from HP Vertica engineers."

On a deeper level, analytics also enables Bailey to identify frequently raised ideas, which can be markers for product and documentation enhancement needs that he can send to the appropriate departments. Alternatively, Get Satisfaction has a tab where users can make formal-enhancement suggestions.

Integrating Salesforce.com

In keeping with the community objective of helping customers, the HP Vertica team was careful not to let the community appear to be a sales or marketing site. So, although HP Vertica uses the Salesforce Cloud product suite for its front-end CRM, including the Sales Cloud, Marketing Cloud, and Service Cloud, its strongest integration between CRM and the Get Satisfaction community is via the Support Cloud. Support-case data can easily be moved or replicated from Get Satisfaction to Salesforce.com when, for instance, a customer request on the community is elevated to a support issue.

But most often Get Satisfaction and Salesforce.com reinforce each other by enabling answers to customer inquiries to be exposed to search engines so that when other customers are making similar inquiries using search, the answers will be available.

Developing a marketplace

One of the first projects HP Vertica wanted to tackle with the community was establishing a marketplace for partners to help in developing the partner ecosystem. A product like HP Vertica can easily be surrounded by plug-ins and apps that enhance the value of the core solution. Planners envisioned a marketplace similar to the AppStore, where customers could research, evaluate, and download accessory solutions.

In the process, HP Vertica would become a platform where customers could easily evaluate product choices, and the community could enable communication between the customers, partners, and HP Vertica. The community would also provide a venue where partners could match the freemium approach initiated by HP Vertica for end customers.

But the partners found that with the core product available as a free download and with free use for databases under a terabyte, they were under the same constraints as HP Vertica for their market outreach: For them, the community became a necessary part of delivering services to technical users in a freemium model.

The community was the obvious first step in the longer-term vision of the marketplace, because it gives users a common place where partners, customers, and potential customers can test, demo, and discuss apps. Just as the community provides a place for core product knowledge exchange, it can also provide the same facility for the partners. But first, the community and the marketplace had to be integrated — that job also went to Bailey.

The marketplace went live in a soft launch in October 2013. The soft launch approach is organic in that partners are adding products as they are ready, which can take time. Some vendors' products fit the freemium download model template, but others don't (HP Vertica is working to get to that point). The division also encourages end users to build products it calls UDXs (user defined extensions), and to place them on the marketplace, as well. But the combination of a soft launch and organic growth has meant a relatively slow deployment. As Bailey says, "People only come when they need something." So critical mass is still building.

Nonetheless, this organic approach seems to be right in line with HP Vertica's leading-with-service-and-support style and with trying to be helpful as the primary strategies for building the community and demonstrating its authenticity. If this were a retail situation things would be different, but the genius in this situation has been in accurately interpreting the setting and being in the moment.

Going live

The eventual goal of preparation and training is to make the new community self-sustaining and independent, not simply going live. That doesn't mean abandonment right after going live either. Get Satisfaction maintains a relationship throughout the life of a community, but the responsibility for communicating and meeting increasingly transfers to the customer.

Chickens or eggs

Going live presents at least one-chicken-or-egg situation: Should the vendor set up the community and then invite people to participate or should the vendor invite trusted customers and partners to help in the setup process? There's no right answer and as it turns out, much depends on the early objective of the community. HP Vertica wanted a community that was service oriented and would offer helpful advice from day one, so the team worked to build content and other facilities that would achieve this goal.

It was a soft launch based on the assumption that the primary reason people would visit the community would be to find answers to technical questions. But this approach neglected another reason people might want to visit and join a community. Sharing is a big part of a successful community but it's not the first thing people think of doing in a new community. People didn't know about the community unless they were searching for answers in a search engine or if they were visiting the HP Vertica site.

After about four weeks of relatively slow adoption, which nonetheless enabled the team to continue to improve the site, the team went into recruitment mode. "We put a community tab on our website and sent an email to our customers," Sandahl says. They also put a banner ad on their website. "That's when we really saw people start to get interested."

Daily meetings

Jenkins held daily meetings with the HP Vertica team for the first few weeks after the live date. The meetings were about 20 minutes long "We looked at the topics that came in from the last day and we looked at how people responded to them," Jenkins says. She was looking for signs that the team was acting in a community-oriented way — using the right language, demonstrating friendliness and transparency — the things a community has to display. These meetings have become a part of the HP Vertica team's internal culture of providing transparency and self-examination to ensure smooth operation.

Two-month health checks

Many subscription companies have adopted the idea of actively working for customer success with their products and services, which often boils down to analyzing metrics and applying personal expertise where needed. For Get Satisfaction, it also means monitoring customers and holding review meetings every couple of months to ensure that lessons learned continue to be applied and to understand future requirements. Subscription companies have learned, sometimes the hard way, that waiting for a customer to raise a hand and ask for assistance might be waiting too long. Once frustration sets in, it's hard to counter. Jenkins calls these meetings health checks, because their emphasis is on reinforcing good ideas and promoting new ones. The Get Satisfaction support team is always available to deal with service issues that come up, but the health check is a proactive part of the service.

The team tracks an array of issues related to community success, such as the ecosystem of other social tools in use and how they interact with each other. Jenkins has a list of her own community-success appraisals, including how customers are interacting with each other; how the community fits into that; how it has configured the application; and if all the product's features being used.

For example, Jenkins says, "A healthy community needs to have a few things, such as peer-to-peer interaction. You don't want it to just be all company-to-customer. You want customer-to-customer, too." When customers discuss things among themselves it's like an idea or several are distilled through activities that a vendor alone couldn't perform, because the vendor's mindset might not even countenance that point of view. So, customer-to-customer interaction is very important and, not surprisingly, it's one of the things a health check analyzes.

"We also look at metrics," Jenkins says. Jenkins and Sandahl rely on Bailey's reports during health checks to monitor performance and identify tweaks.

Do's and Don'ts for Managed Communities

HP Vertica's Managed Community from Get Satisfaction has been a big success. It's engaging customers and introducing users to each other in a virtuous cycle that couldn't be more different from the old-school situation found at too many Sucks-and-sentiment sites. This managed community is a good example of both the AKP in action and the value of understanding customer moments of truth and being present for them. As the Anna Karenina Principle implies, you'll never get to a state of perfection where there are no issues and all customers are happy, but a well-run community is the next best thing. It seeks out opportunities to repair processes that might be going off track. Let's look at a few do's and don'ts for running a successful community.

Do

- Follow the guidelines for setting up and running a
  Managed Community that we discussed in Chapter 7. If
  your aspirations and purpose are clear and your early

members are on the same page, success will come more easily.

- Be clear about your community's charter and the scope of its reach. You might discover that your business needs multiple communities to handle all its customers, brands, market segments, etc. Uncovering a new use for communities in your business will cost a little cash, but this is a good problem to have. It means another opportunity to connect with customers to learn from them, bond, and ultimately, sell more or increase share. It will also reduce the nasty surprise of churn.

- Ensure to promote an atmosphere of trust and tolerance. Nothing makes people clam up faster or not come back than having some person become loud and obstreperous. Remember, it's the CM's job to keep things fun, but businesslike.

- Provide meaningful activities for people to participate in or they'll drift away.

- Provide feedback frequently. Members will enjoy knowing what the group thinks, and that's something you can share once you've collected some data and performed some analysis. Sharing is a good way to get people talking again to refine what they meant. You'll be collecting additional ideas that fine-tune your inquiry. You'll also be providing an easy reward for participating.

- Consider the appropriate business processes that might be kicked off from the community. Nothing Big Brotherish but if someone is obviously in need of some kind of help a referral to a department within the company will be appreciated and, importantly, noticed.

Don't

- Don't worry about participation rates. The old 80/20 rule applies. In a managed community people are free to come and go, and many will stand by and watch if they have nothing to add or if an issue doesn't concern them. But the fact that they come to the community means they get something from the experience. They will talk when they have something to say.

- Don't worry if a conversation goes sideways occasionally, especially when you're getting started. People are getting to know one another, so some amount of extra conversation is bound to happen. But keep an eye on the drift and be ready to judiciously reel it back in when it drifts too far. Think about equipoise, an athlete's balanced state of alert-but-relaxed between plays. It's the perfect model.

- Don't be afraid of offering a little praise or a small reward from time to time. There's a fine line that your community manager will need to draw. A little praise will go a long way in promoting good feeling and participation in your community. Acknowledgements and status are cheap or free, but they are also powerful motivators for people to turn their altruistic impulses to more positive actions.

Consider gamification, badges, and rewards for participation

One of the easiest rewards you can provide is a badge an icon that says this person does something well and often. It's part of gamification and it is remarkably effective at promoting positive behaviors.

The line you need to draw for rewards is between tangible value and status. Something of value like $100 isn't ideal for two reasons. First, it promotes pay-for-praise, which can corrode a community's cohesion. The community has to be seen by all members as a boat that everyone is rowing. You need to promote the community's shared purpose and responsibility.

The second reason to avoid monetary rewards is that there's little opportunity to show objectively that the reward is merited. The rewards that come from you represents your subjective opinion. A better approach is to provide status gleaned from the other community members. Recently, many businesses have been using gamification to engage customers in various activities, such as participating in communities, offering peer support, and writing help tips for their knowledge bases. You can see the value provided for such member-donated services and a reward like a badge appropriately provides acknowledgement and status.

I can't do better than turn to Lori Jenkins for the last word on relationships and rewards: "I used to be a teacher and I've taught kids and adults. And it's the same no matter who is being recognized. People love to be rewarded and appreciated, especially publicly. I think in terms of human behavior, it's exactly the same with adults and kids." There's a practical side to this also: "You also want to create a sticky situation — if I participate, I want to be recognized for it and I want to come back and see what people are talking about and how they're interacting with my content."

Jenkins's recommendation for making awards is simple. Titles and badges are big deals in a community and they should be treated accordingly. She advises, "When someone becomes a champion, announce it to the whole community. It's amazing what it does, even for grown-ups. You'll be really surprised."

SftC Takeaways

1. The Managed Community is the workhorse for most community applications.

2. How HP engaged with Get Satisfaction to build a robust Managed Community.

3. Do's and Don'ts for Managed Communities.

Managed Communities provide a great deal of insight into customers' behaviors. In Chapter 9 we look at Mediated Communities, which provide insight into their motivations.

Chapter Nine

Communispace: A Mediated Community

A Mediated Community operates most like a laboratory and the comparison between Customer Science and sociology can be seen most easily here. Mediated communities are specifically designed to research ideas with selected groups. Moreover, they seek to capture and understand the emotional component of customer behavior to learn about why customers behave in particular ways. Discovering customers' behaviors and learning why they behave as they do are powerful tools for vendors attempting to penetrate new markets and design new products. Often those reasons are not apparent but once uncovered they can pinpoint moments of truth.

A Mediated Community is the highpoint of Customer Science because it is designed specifically to research ideas with specific groups. A Managed community generates a lot of numeric data from a cross section of customers. But a Mediated community hand selects specific people whose attributes, e.g., job titles, roles, experience, give their ideas great authority. As you will see, when researching abstract concepts it is often helpful to leverage a community's storytelling capabilities.

Communispace, a Social Laboratory

Boston-based Communispace was one of the first movers in the social-media space (see Chapter 4). But rather than going retail and enlisting millions of users in sprawling networks or trying to leverage an advertising business model as many social networks have done, the company built a unique practice by uncovering the wisdom that only individuals can provide while giving context to the big data that inundates us. Again, it's a question of horses for courses: Communispace's mediated approach might not be the right community approach for all conditions but it has a lock on situations where organizations simply have to know what customers actually think, including the emotions behind the thoughts.

Operating a Communispace community in some ways mirrors active sociology research. We touched on sociology in Chapter 6 but now it's time to make more connections between sociology and the emerging phenomenon called Customer Science. Here's a quick review: Sociology tries to identify why people do what they do and sociologists divide the answers into the two broad categories of structure and agency. Structure deals with how people might behave in well-defined (or structured) social situations by conforming to norms; agency is a way of describing an individual taking responsibility for acting outside of a structured situation.

It's not a question of which is better or right. It's yet another example of horses for courses. Each offers a window into human nature. My impression of Communispace communities is that they study the emotions causing people to either take agency (and perhaps act independently) or make a more structured response to a novel situation.

Compare this with a pure big-data approach that tries statistically to correlate behaviors using retrospective customer-behavior data analysis. Statistical approaches are fine but too often users stop once they've discovered a correlation and forget to ask if the correlation is causative. Using both big data and delving into the emotional response to identify the whys of customer behavior can forge deep connections that help vendors to understand not only what *is* but also what could *be*. This approach attaches meaning to statistical facts and can identify the reasons for behaviors, the causation. In the process we promote simple data into actionable knowledge. When that happens it can trigger a vendor's empathetic response to customers' needs that go well beyond a product offering, which defines moments of truth. When vendors meet customers in moments of truth one important (and desired) result is bonding.

Big data

Perhaps you've heard the saying *correlation does not equal causation*. It means that simply because there may be a statistical link between two things, it's not certain that one causes the other. A folksy expression of this phenomenon is *the rooster taking credit for the sunrise*. A rooster might crow at the right time (correlation) but the sun would rise regardless (no causation). This is the increasing dilemma of big data — the data might tell us there is a correlation in some kind of customer behavior, but the reality may be that there is little or no causation. Alternatively, the causation might be buried beneath multiple layers of behavior and data, and asking customers directly about how they feel under certain circumstances may be the only way to relate the correlation to causation.

Given this, it should not be surprising that upwards of 70 percent of new product introductions each year fail — despite the best market research and testing, the majority of new products miss the mark. It's been this way for a long time because collecting customer input about feelings and experiences has been so labor intensive and time consuming that innovators have frequently had to make assumptions about them just to get products out the door.

The Uses for Communispace Communities

Communispace cofounder and SVP of innovation and design Julie Wittes Schlack writes on the Communispace blog[2] that there are four key areas in which mediated communities like those offered by Communispace can make a big difference in a vendor's go-to-market strategy. Here, my take on four important points:

1. **Uncovering unmet needs and moments of truth.** All vendors want to uncover unmet customer needs that they can uniquely fill. Meeting these needs is the source of vendor differentiation and high profit, which is a principle reason vendors are so eager to bring new products to market. But new-product introductions often suffer from one or more of the

following shortcomings, which you might be tempted to call the antithesis of right product, right place, right time. They lack differentiation, have inappropriate pricing, and garbled messaging. Involving customers in these fundamental product decisions using a mediated community can do a lot to reduce the failure rate.

2. **Capturing new audiences.** If a business can't always innovate around unmet needs, it can attempt to reach new audiences with its existing products, which is still great for growing market share. Wittes Schlack writes that this was the situation Charles Schwab found itself in a few years ago. "It needed to connect with future investors while they were still young," she says, "before they had the investable income that would make them part of Schwab's traditional client base." The solution was a community that enabled Schwab to gain a deep understanding of gen-x consumers. Schwab and the community were able to cocreate a new product that met the generation's needs and brought it into a relationship with the brand.

3. **Product and campaign launches**. Here a community of existing and prospective users can provide insights about all aspects of a new campaign, including teaser campaigns, messaging, packaging and more, depending on the type of product.

4. **Crisis management**. The United Breaks Guitars incident could have been better managed had there been a fast, easy, and economical approach to gauging the public's reaction. Had United been able to ask a customer community for its opinions prior to Dave Carroll's patience reaching its limit, the airline might have been able to contain the damage. Even if you believe that the best way to avoid a crisis situation is to be more proactive in the first place, you can't plan for every contingency. Having a community that you can quickly query about out-of-the-ordinary

situations as a regular part of your marketing outreach can be worth a lot.

Storytelling — How These Communities Work

Communispace communities are not survey-taking machines that spit out a continuous supply of data based on a scale of one-to-five, plus NA. Nor are they the reduction of the social stream you see in Ad Hoc communities. Those two approaches are valid in the right situations, but they aren't the best fit when you want to know how people feel and what motivates them in a moment of truth.

Communispace communities capture a great deal of customer data but not only the backward-looking data of a survey that fuels an analytics engine. That data, big data, is important, too, but to better inform it, Communispace communities capture individuals' nuances and the reasons they act.

For instance, backward-looking behavioral-data analysis can tell you unambiguously who bought what (and famously, that individuals or companies that bought product A also bought product B). But is this causation or merely correlation? To find out, you need to ask a few real customers, which turns out to be easier than it sounds.

Unlike conventional data-gathering approaches, Communispace communities cultivate knowledge about customers. The primary tool for cultivating knowledge that Communispace communities draw on is storytelling. People understand narratives, perhaps better than numbers. People's intuitive understanding of stories makes a Communispace community powerful. Communispace helps companies to understand their customers' stories and to mine those stories for the deeper emotional drivers that provide keys to understanding unmet needs, positioning a solution that meets a new customer's requirements, whatever those requirements are, and to recognizing what's important in a crisis and what is extraneous.

There are stories and there are *stories*. Stories affect us on a deeper level than mere data, says Communispace's Hessan: "High-impact stories pique the interest of decision makers and alter our

145

perceptions and assumptions, revealing the real meaning behind the information we have learned. And by allowing businesses' decision makers to better understand their customers stories provide needed insight to help move business confidently in the right direction." Here are her recommendations for leveraging communities.[3]

1. Get personal and build relationships.
2. Plan deliberately and explore from different angles.
3. Use human intuition to find the story that matters.
4. Evoke emotions that inspire action.

Let's explore them in detail.

Get personal

Building relationships means building the trust that people first need before they can reveal their innermost thoughts, the kind that describe unmet needs, hopes, and dreams. This is the same idea of trust we started with in Chapter 8 when we discussed setting up a community. It turns out that no matter what kind of community you decide to use or what its objectives might be, if you expect people to invest their time and bare their souls, you have to first promote a trusting environment. It's what Get Satisfaction did with HP and it's what Communispace does, too. It's one of the big differences between Ad Hoc Communities where people freely vent onto social networks, sentiment, and sucks sites (perhaps a little too freely). There they bare their souls but often the venting is not measured or balanced.

Plan deliberately

At the same time, work to ditch your assumptions about what appears to have worked before. If you ask people to answer a survey, they'll most likely answer in a thoughtful, logical, and intelligent manner that's devoid of the emotional content you want to explore. That's why Communispace uses activities. For example, a Communispace CM helping to develop a new candy bar wouldn't ask, "How many peanuts would you like in every bite?" or "On a scale of 1 to 5 with 5 being 'I really like this' and 1 meaning 'I don't care for this at all,' please rate your favorite chocolate — white, milk, or dark." Instead, the CM may build an activity that asks the members to describe their ideal candy bar. It's an open-ended task that leaves everything up to the member to determine. The member is completely free to tap into a best memory or deepest desire for a candy bar (regardless of brand or other limitations), and that's what you want. Of course, Communispace also has survey capability. But the biggest insights often emerge from the open-ended question that's often last in a survey, "What else do you have to tell us?" So why not ask open-ended questions first?

Use human intuition

Throughout *Solve for the Customer*, we emphasize quantitative data analysis but good research involves both the quantitative and the qualitative. Rather than simply finding some statistical mean or stack ranking the responses to the candy-bar research above (52 percent liked peanuts with an average of 3.2 per bite, 63 percent liked milk chocolate best, etc.) use your human intelligence to weight the data looking for connections that people are best at finding.

Hessan relates a compelling story about how U.K. Telecom Everything Everywhere (EE) leveraged the findings from its community. "EE already knew that customers loved their mobile phones. But only after hearing consumers share personal stories of those dreadful 'uh-oh' moments when they dropped their phone in a toilet or lost it in a taxicab did EE truly understand that it wasn't the physical phones that people cared about, it was everything inside them: pictures, funny videos, personal contact lists, important meetings, and amusing text exchanges with friends. EE executives intuitively related to that sinking feeling of losing precious memories and information in an instant of human error. Out of this understanding was born the Clone Phone, EE's service solution to data backup, storage, and even phone replacement guaranteed within 24 hours. The new service was an instant hit: More than 250,000 Clone Phone subscribers signed up in the first six months."

Evoke emotions

The power of a good story is that it cuts through the logical and quantitative structures that govern big parts of our lives. Stories surface emotional responses in a memorable way. Executives and employees that derive lessons from good stories don't need to be told twice. A good customer story can have a chain reaction throughout an organization.

Another Communispace community advantage is that it lets people interact over an idea, and a concept can mature in the process into something more fully formed than simply knowing that a new chocolate bar with peanuts might appeal to a certain population. You might be able to market a new product but it's the stories that uncover the emotional link that will help you sell it.

MetLife is another Communispace client. The $60-plus billion colossus (it is 42 on the 2014 Fortune 500 list of large American companies) sells insurance in more than 60 countries and serves customers across product lines as diverse as health and dental care to annuities and, of course, life insurance.

Senior Vice President and Chief Customer Officer Claire Burns discussed storytelling in a research interview for *Solve for the Customer,* In her example she said, "We had the community do an exercise where they wrote a letter to a relative about why one might want to buy insurance. The power of these letters was amazing. One that I've shared with our audiences frequently, involves a sister writing to her brother saying, 'Wouldn't our lives have been different if Dad had life insurance? We wouldn't have been going hungry every week. Our Mom wouldn't have had to work two jobs.' It was a heart-wrenching story [and] it's amazing what you get when you ask."

Horses for Courses

Customer engagement, customer centricity, customer experience — we use a lot of words to describe the effort to place customers in the center of focus in our businesses. And while we mostly understand the importance of this effort, results can prove elusive unless you start with a disciplined plan and a balanced view of people, process, and technology. Attempts to focus on one to the exclusion of the others almost always ends in failure and frustration. But all this is a warm-up for the next phase in customer relationships.

SftC Takeaways

1. Understanding the emotional component of customer behavior can reveal the causation, the why, of their behaviors.

2. Storytelling is an important tool for getting to the why.

3. Community can be seen as a customer laboratory for this important research.

Chapter 10 discusses what happens when the customer can only give a limited range of input, for example, when the primary customer is a machine.

Chapter Ten
The Future of Community

Customer Science assumes, along with "The Culture Code," that quirky humans are the actors in the vendor-customer relationship. But what happens when machines begin to play the role of primary consumer? The ideas developed in Customer Science apply equally well in the Internet of Things (IoT).

There are two important questions driving the discussion about the future of community: Who will the customer be? and How will the vendor communicate? The answers are not as obvious as they might seem because we're in the early stages of the smart-machines rollout. The smart machines of the near future are devices much like the cars and appliances on the market now, but they'll have computer intelligence and networking built in like never before. They will communicate directly with other machines using machine-to-machine interfaces now coming to market. They'll also absorb customer data as a matter of course without needing any special protocols, and they'll store it in large databases for analysis and retrieval at critical times. These are the machines that will augment human intelligence in ways that Garry Kasparov observed and Brynjolfsson and McAfee envision (see Chapter 5).

Consider these smart machines already on the market:

1. Your car probably has multiple sensors built into it that can monitor all kinds of activity and alert you to pending needs for maintenance. Sometimes these sensors also alert a dealer or mechanic. The next iteration of car might look like Google Car, which drives itself using a variety of GPS and sensing technologies to keep the car on the road and unscratched in traffic.

2. Philips makes an ultrasound system for hospital use that is wired directly to the manufacturer to instantly assist and troubleshoot technical and operational issues whenever needed.

3. General Electric is adding smarts to its jet aircraft engines that monitor performance and transmit data in real time to engineers on the ground to inform them whether or not the engine is running up to specifications. With that information airlines can depot parts and adjust schedules or arrange to reroute customers in case of maintenance delays.

Vendors are identifying major moments of truth in all these cases and ensuring that they can insert themselves seamlessly into the customer consciousness at critical junctures. Some of these moments of truth are uncovered through communities, but in other cases it's a matter of analyzing the data stream directly from the machine that provides the information. Vendors are also uncovering additional moments of truth and opportunities to be of service in the process. When vendors can behave this way, customers are more likely to see them as partners, not simply potential consumers for the next cross sell.

The customer's role will not likely change much but a new level of abstraction will come into play. In Chapter 2 we discussed the difference between a customer and a consumer and concluded that *customers* make the decisions and participate in virtuous cycles. *Consumers* are simply on the receiving end of a supply chain. That's still true but it's likely that soon, the buying persona will be a consumer in the form of a smart machine that happens to be owned by your customer. If a vendor manages the relationship correctly by deploying the systems and processes that collect data from smart-machine consumers, that vendor will be able to present evidence for the next sale to the customer. The vendor will not longer have to rely on sales mind games, such as offering discounting schemes, to get the next order. The next order will be a foregone conclusion, much like it is in the subscription economy. When that happens, vendors will become full partners with their customers.

Vendors will need systems of engagement unlike ones they've seen before to play in this new world. Tomorrow's systems of engagement will be designed to support advanced business processes that involve people — they won't be automated away — as well as smart machines. Those systems will progress beyond the transaction automation we see today, and will have built-in workflow, collaboration, analytics, and other specialty applications, which will transform mere transactions into processes. They'll also require code-generation capabilities that enable a vendor's IT department to generate apps for every platform relevant to the business, from the desktop to the palm (and even wearable devices). A key ability of these systems will be to generate apps quickly at any time to support changing business requirements.

The targets of this code generation will likely be conventional desktop and laptop systems and their browsers, plus the same functionality for tablets and handheld devices with several operating-system choices. We don't know what the hot wearables will be or how they'll be integrated into the process landscape, but we can forecast that they'll depend on a platform's generating capability.

Increasingly, vendors will need to analyze customer data to understand things like uptake, use, and financial trends. For some vendors this will be easy — it's an extension of what they planned for when they built their first communities and started listening to customers.

Let's look at a prosaic domestic appliance — a reach-in freezer — and a unique application that New England BioLabs designed for it using the Salesforce1 application platform from Salesforce.com. You'll get a sense of how pervasive and valuable the machine-to-machine interface is becoming to business.

New England BioLabs, Inc.

New England BioLabs, Inc. (NEB) was founded in the mid-1970s as a collective of scientists committed to developing innovative products for the life-sciences industry. Today NEB is a recognized world leader in the discovery, development, and commercialization of recombinant and native enzymes for genomic research[i].

The company earned its reputation developing, isolating, and packaging enzymes that enable scientists to cut RNA and DNA strands at specific points to isolate sections of genetic material that code for specific proteins in cells. Using these molecules, scientists can study how genes are expressed in both health and disease states. This kind of research has led to many of the blockbuster new drugs and biologic based medical treatments on the market today.

This biomedical research is often carried out in a university or university medical center setting by medical doctors and Ph.D. scientists. Because the enzymes and other reagents the company sells are biologically active — their functions as enzymes are preserved even when they're outside of living cells — NEB delivers many of them frozen. Researchers return them to room temperature or warmer to use them in research experiments.

NEB understands its customers' moments of truth and like any vendor, the company wants to meet its customers' expectations. For NEB that means being in the test tube with biologically active reagents whenever the scientist wants to run an experiment. Since NEB is a company primarily comprising scientists serving other scientists, it has been relatively easy for it to cater to its clientele. Very often a researcher can contact a NEB scientist to discuss how a reagent is made or its optimal use, as well as to trouble shoot an experiment.

As a 40-plus year-old company, NEB has aspects of its business that have been dictated by IT constraints as technology has evolved. Like many companies, that means it has operations silos in sales, marketing, and service. NEB CIO Ken Grady saw this when he joined the company and wanted to help integrate functions at the IT level to provide a better return on the IT investment, as well as to improve the ways that NEB reached out to its customers.

NEB implemented Salesforce.com CRM about two years ago for sales, marketing, and service, which put its front-office operations on a single platform and enabled the major departments to share data better (thus informing all its customer-facing business processes).

In an interview with Grady for *Solve for the Customer*, he says that before implementing Salesforce.com, "We weren't doing as good a job as we wanted to of bringing all the customer touchpoints together where we had a true 360-degree picture of the customer interaction. Whether customers call us about buying more products or call with a scientific question or with collaboration possibilities or to check on their invoice, we wanted to do a better job in all of those things."

But even with a full Salesforce.com implementation, there was more to do and Grady and his colleagues were intrigued by the possibilities inherent in the powerful application platform Salesforce1, which Salesforce CRM is built on. NEB began to leverage the platform for other IT purposes, such as its freezer program.

The Program

NEB has a catalogue business from which customers locate and order specific enzymes and reagents. It operates a freezer program, a consignment business in which NEB positions about 80 of its most popular products at a customer's location. Researchers can have access to needed reagents to perform experiments without having to wait for an overnight shipment.

The freezer program dates to the 1980s and is very popular, spawning imitations by NEB's competition. Competition drives these vendors to search for new products and services, and for ways to deliver them. If a researcher is working on an experiment targeting cancer cells in combination, for example, NEB's research scientists may be able to collaborate with them to understand which reagents in what quantities would best support the effort. But it's not top of mind for researchers to run to suppliers to test ideas all the time; a company first has to understand customers by collecting use data before it can attempt to be in the moment of truth.

Biomedical research happens at its own pace. Sometimes an experiment might run around the clock — researchers need reagents that are available to them at any time. For decades the NEB solution had been to place a freezer full of reagents — solutions and enzymes, for instance — close to customers but limitations imposed by then state-of-the-art technology didn't bring the freezers right into the lab. The freezers were often kept in a central location like a university's central-stores building; researchers would typically need to cross campus to pick up reagents, and sometimes a particular reagent wasn't available (leading to the need to ship an order overnight). The process was completely manual: A central store kept inventory and periodically it was replenished and invoices were sent to the researchers who bought and used the products. The freezer program was a close, but not an optimal, solution.

While researchers might work around the clock, central stores at most universities keep more regular hours, so relying on them for reagents was less than optimal. But the central location was necessary to support the given freezer configuration. As Grady describes it the original freezer program, "got us about halfway to the goal of making sure that our reagents — our products — were available whenever the customer wanted."

NEB considered going with a vending-machine approach, but that had several drawbacks, including the freezer's capacity and the fact that it was not connected to the grid. Connection to the Internet was critical for rolling out a new freezer program because it opened the possibility of gathering customer data.

Dreamforce Connection

By 2012 updating the freezer program was top of mind in NEB's IT group; the operating idea was to offer better customer service. Other ideas circulating included the need for bi-directional communication, so that freezers in customer locations could communicate about inventory and status with the manufacturing facility in Massachusetts in real time.

Several members of the NEB IT team accompanied Grady to Dreamforce 2012, the annual Salesforce.com customer conference held in San Francisco, and they were inspired by stories about other vendor experiences. Coca-Cola, whose new vending machine was connected to the Internet, could send its status information to the supplier and store customers' favorite mix recipes in a cloud database so that customers can get their custom flavor anywhere. "In particular we'd seen the GE video where the aircraft engines were sending notifications into Salesforce and saying, 'Hey, I'm in flight now. I'm going to land in San Francisco at SFO in two hours and I need a replacement part, so have one ready for me," Grady says. It didn't take the NEB team long to process that idea and come up with its own for the freezers.

The team happened to be at a bar after having seen the GE video when the idea of the freezer program came up, and in the best tradition of cocktail-napkin engineering, in a few minutes it had sketched out a new freezer and a customer process that went far beyond the consignment model of the 1980s — all the way to being inside a customer's moment of truth.

Grady summarizes the main ideas that came from the impromptu meeting: "We wanted to do it quickly and ensure that it was all tied to using tablet computers. We also put a couple of additional constraints on ourselves, saying it all had to be driven with commercially available parts; we didn't want to have to specially engineer anything. So we were connecting bits that we could get anywhere. It also held down costs." These were important considerations given that NEB does business in many countries with different parts availabilities and different electrical power standards.

Last, the team also wanted the new freezers to be easy to use. "If we have to train somebody in how to use the freezers, we haven't done a good enough job with design," Grady says, "and of course, we've benefited from the fact that we're now all trained to self-checkout at the grocery store or check-in on your airplane by yourself."

All of these design criteria are examples of NEB–customer moments of truth captured over years of listening. It paid off because the criteria enabled the IT team to move the freezers out of central stores and closer to NEB's actual customers. The new design criteria also reduced the constraints imposed by the operating hours of central stores in some locations.

NEB started with a standard Windows tablet, Grady says: "And we took the USB controllers for a barcode reader and thermometer and other parts, and we tied them all together and developed an app-like interface using Salesforce1's application development and generation tools."

The new freezer works like this: A researcher types in an access code on the tablet and the freezer unlocks, enabling the researcher to remove vials of reagents. The researcher scans the vials' bar codes and the tablet sends this information to the NEB ERP system, which calculates the products' prices referencing the customer's volume price list. A periodic invoice is later sent to the researcher or university, as appropriate.

Among the benefits of this approach, Grady says, are that NEB gets "real time feedback — it's not a feed, it's actually tied to the cloud. When you log in you're validating against your Salesforce customer number in our organization. And you get your price." That's a big success but it's not the end of the story.

Going Farther

A vendor must find ways to collect relevant data and make logical inferences to get to a customer's moments of truth — that's where analytics comes in. The improved freezers gave NEB a window into the research its customers were doing that was hard to get any other way. The data trail that showed what reagents each researcher was using proved to be a rich source for analyzing product uptake, and with the help of some intuitive understanding from the scientists at NEB, has resulted in new collaboration opportunities.

"If we know that you're taking out certain products and we just developed a new protocol for them," Grady says, "we can send you an email with that protocol so that we give you information that's relevant to you. We also get more information: If people are taking out certain combinations of products, that might tell us something about a new application they're working on that we may optimize for them. If you're targeting cancer cells in a certain combination, maybe we can optimize a product for that research."

Such close research support has rarely been done like this in the field. With a product catalog containing more than 2,000 items, there is a reasonable chance that a researcher may not be aware of some combinations or the availability of certain reagents that could make a difference in that researcher's work.

The old freezer program could provide only aggregate data about how a whole institution may be consuming products. That's not fine grained enough for most circumstances today. According to Grady, the former freezer program had aspects of an old Coca-Cola vending machine: "All a vendor can tell is that somebody's drinking a lot of Diet Coke, but no idea who's drinking it.

"Now we can actually talk to the researcher down at the bench level," Grady says, "and we can say, 'It looks like you're having a challenge cloning this particular protein that has a particular stretch of DNA that has a high GC (guanine and cytosine, which are types of nucleotides) content. Well, we have a product that's optimized for that. Let me show that to you.'" This kind of specificity makes for higher-value customer relationships. "We actually have the information that enables us to have that conversation," Grady says. "That's a much more useful and intelligent conversation than you could have simply knowing that somebody in this account is using a lot of this product."

Of equal importance is NEB's ability to monitor the temperature inside its freezers and the status of the door lock, which can help manage quality control and protect stock. Imagine a scenario in which the temperature in a freezer begins to rise, for example, setting off an alert at NEB that prompts a phone call to a location manager or user to check the freezer door.

Road map

Grady plans to replace all of the old freezers at customer locations with the new intelligent models. New freezers have been distributed to a handful of customer sites and NEB has been able to iterate from version 1 to version 2 of the user interface in only a few months, thanks to the Salesforce1 platform. As it considers future iterations of the product, Grady's team is contemplating how it can place freezers in locations where there is no Internet service. One approach, which Grady refers to as the Fitbit model, stores order information on a researcher's phone through a Bluetooth connection. The phone then sends the information to NEB later through Wi-Fi or 3G/4G networking.

NEB's moments of truth

Grady has not thought about all this as being in a series of moments of truth, so I asked him it is. "Absolutely," he says. "That's just one example and there are other examples where we can say, 'Hey, now we know better. We understand better how you're using our products, and that allows us to guide you to the product that will work best for you.'"

"That's all we ever want as customers, right? It doesn't matter if we're talking about the lab and professional use or [about] home use. We want the product that works best for our needs. The better we understand the needs, the better we can point you in the right direction."

The Second Machine Age

Let's consider how the NEB scenario fits into the future we envision for people, process, technology, and smart machines. As machines gain a kind of intelligence that enables smarter business processes, one might think that people will be automated out of the picture. That's not Brynjolfsson and McAfee's conclusion (see Chapter 5). They see a different future, one in which the increased reliance on data and analytics gives businesses greater flexibility to place employees into situations — moments of truth, if you like — where only a human intellect can make the right decisions and offer the right service, product, or support.

You can see this taking shape in the way that the data stream from the NEB freezers informs the vendor about possible customer needs. Armed with specific information, NEB scientists can focus their attention where it will do both the business and the customer the most good. As Kasparov wrote, "Weak human + machine + better process was superior to a strong computer alone and, more remarkably, superior to a strong human + machine + inferior process."[2] This should reassure anyone contemplating how people fit into an increasingly automated world. The answer is (as it always has been) a mix of people, process, technology (and now smart machines), which open up greater opportunities. A freezer is a lot less complex than a jet engine; using it as a data-collection device can still yield impressive new opportunities to improve business processes and can drive the kinds of results that contribute to those all important customer bonds.

The Importance of Platform

For modern business applications to support customer moments of truth, we'll need far more than simple database applications and row-and column-reports. Modern business approaches require much more, including workflow, collaboration, multiple hardware-and-operating system deployments, and, of course, analytics. All this must be built in, not layered onto conventional applications.

But platform's central importance doesn't stop with all the outbound capabilities designed to deliver the right messages to customers at the right time. Platform tools also include workflow and journey mapping tools that help businesses model moments of truth so that they can generate the necessary apps that will in many cases be in those moments with customers. Modeling tools represent the last leg in a virtuous circle that enables a business to apply its new knowledge, derived through analytics, back to the customer. This strongly suggests that application platforms will not just be something nice to have, they'll be business necessities going forward.

We've been discussing big data collection, analytics, rapid application development and deployment throughout *Solve for the Customer* in much the same ways we have for decades, as separate ideas. The result leaves us with incremental improvements in parts of front-office business but has so far prevented the major improvements that many have sought.

SftC Takeaways

1. Consider future communities of machines. The data gathering and analysis developed today will pay big dividends in the IoT.

2. Devices can't talk (yet), but they can still send useful data that you can turn into knowledge and profit.

3. How New England BioLabs leverages a variety of technologies to improve business processes and customer outreach.

4. A new formulation for People, Process, and Technology.

Major improvement comes from using all of these new capabilities in new ways that can more fully leverage their benefits and that requires a new, overarching idea. Customer Science is that idea that relies on platform technology to integrate the individual tools with a statistical orientation of continuous improvement — what the Japanese call *kaizen*.

Chapter Eleven

Customer Science

After collecting and analyzing all your inbound customer-communication data, you know what your moments of truth are. Based on your metrics you can see clearly how well your organization tracks to your goals. The next task is to apply all this new knowledge to outbound communications with your customers. But how do you reach out to them?

For too long the answer to that question has been to spray and pray with social media. That is a misuse of the tools. Social is supposed to give you the ability to have real relationships — a company with thousands of customers can't have *personal* relationships with customers but it can have *real* relationships. This means being authentically present within customers' moments of truth. Whether your intelligent software performs the steps of the relationship or your people do is not the issue, authenticity is. Spray and pray is not authentic.

For example, a system that suggests condoms as substitutes for antacids is inauthentic but so is having real people stonewall a damage claim; likewise for treating your customer base as nothing more than a place in Philadelphia where you mine money. Authenticity means dealing with it all. When you think about it, the Anna Karenina Principle is about authenticity. If one of your customer-facing process cascades break and you either don't know about it or fail to repair it, you are inauthentic and your customers will know.

New technology, new processes, and new science

The modern assortment of technology available to front office business practitioners is amazing. It enables us to think differently about our business processes and to invent new ways to interact with our customers. But if we use the new tools in business-as-usual processes, we'll fail to gain the benefits that our vendors promise.

For many years we've accumulated a huge assortment of front-office tools that vendors have promised would help us accelerate business, cut costs, and improve our customer relationships. They've all worked to a degree, but they have failed at most of it because their approaches assume that problems have a single solution. We like the simplicity of a one-and-done solution, but as the Anna Karenina Principle shows, there are many ways that a cascade can go sideways and a single solution won't fix every instance.

If every unhappy family (or customer) is unhappy in its own way, the idea of a cure-all is a pipe dream. But as with unhappy families, uncovering the point of a process failure can help an unhappy customer. Customer Science is an organized approach to discovering moments of truth and our failure points. It employs the Anna Karenina Principle and uses many of the new front-office tools and enables us to continuously improve front office business.

Customer Science is a virtuous circle related to sociology (see Chapter 6) that starts from the customer and travels to the vendor and then back to the customer. If you doubt that we're at the point of declaring a new front office business science, consider the following.

Chaos and Science

A science is an organized framework for dealing with the issues particular to a line of inquiry. Importantly, the framework can be used to identify solutions to problems that may not have existed when the science was developed. Understanding gravity and the equations that explain it enables us to predict the free fall of an object. If you add a little more math you can calculate trajectories of anything from a baseball to a rocket.

Isaac Newton didn't know anything about rockets when he developed calculus and mechanics, but his new science perfectly explained how rockets travel today. Similarly, early chemists, such as Boyle, Priestly, and Lavoisier, didn't have a clue that their research would someday enable us to make things like tires, polymers, and pharmaceuticals. But the laws and relationships among elements that they discovered govern our understanding of chemistry today. And Darwin figured out a lot about biology and inheritance without knowing about genes and genetics.

Social sciences, including Customer Science, have the same predictive value with the caveat that because they deal with a bell curve, we have to consider aggregate behavior and assign probabilities to individual circumstances. Customer Science will help us improve our customer-facing processes regardless of how unique our businesses are.

The road to Customer Science is the same one traveled by every science. First, chaos reigns and there is no differentiation between, for example, astrology and astronomy or alchemy and chemistry. Eventually people begin to apply math to identify patterns. Sometimes, they have to invent a branch of mathematics to prove the science; Newton invented calculus on his way to describing modern mechanics. (For a detailed description of how chaos gives rise to science, see Thomas Kuhn's *The Structure of Scientific Revolutions*.[1])

Statistics made modern social sciences possible; from economics to political science to sociology, social sciences rely on the bell curve and statistics. Interestingly statistics arrived on the scene well before social sciences began to evolve. In the mid-19th century when statistical analysis was first applied to data about social problems like poverty in urban England, the results surprised and embarrassed the government, causing Prime Minister Disraeli to utter his famous dictum that there are three kinds of lies: "lies, damn lies, and statistics." Still statistical analysis of population data is the heart of multiple social sciences today and I believe we should add another discipline to the list, Customer Science.

Customer Science has been an elusive idea for a very long time in part because the pace of business was so slow that many other things clouded our observations. We didn't have enough data to evaluate and if we did have enough, we didn't have sufficient computational power to perform a timely analysis. Both those limitations ended with the big data and analytics revolution of the last few years. It's a paradox that we have had statistics for centuries that we have applied to social problems to good effect, but that we rarely have applied statistics to the vendor-customer relationships.

We receive the benefit of social science work (and statistics) every time we hear a fact about diet, exercise, and longevity in the popular press. In the Framingham Heart Study that began in 1948, for example, medical researchers have studied cohorts of people over decades to ascertain the affects of diet and exercise on heart health and longevity. In 1960 findings from the study first brought our attention to the dangers of cigarette smoking; in every decade since then the study has provided new insights based on statistical analysis of collected data.

Customer Science can affect business activity by enabling us to almost immediately make deductions from the large volume of data and the short duration of most business processes using many of the same analytic techniques — plus the speed of the Internet.

It's important to understand that all the problems encompassed by a science are not solved at the moment it coalesces. But importantly, a new scientific paradigm provides a frame for current and future researchers to understand which problems can be addressed by the science and which ones can't. This is the state of Customer Science today.

Customer Science has not addressed every possible issue for every company in vendor-customer relationships and it probably never will. But the existence of new tools and new paradigms pushes us farther and brings new challenges into focus. Customer Science has finally provided a framework to work in; it shows us that the unique customer situations of every business can yield to a systematic attempt at a resolution. Journey maps are a key component of the system because they help reduce business chaos, replacing it with automated, precise, and repeatable processes.

Journey maps

Journey maps were a marketing innovation but they are rapidly invading all facets of front-office business. The journey map enables companies to structure business processes around moments of truth. Think of a journey map as a big white board for documenting and modeling the Anna Karenina cascade and then some. A journey map is a valuable tool because in addition to helping to model a process as it is, the journey map also enables users to see the places where a customer facing process might break down. Journey maps have four uses:

1. They help users to model existing customer-facing processes around moments of truth so that a business can determine the adequacy of its coverage.

2. They also help to uncover additional process steps or whole processes that may have been unknown prior to modeling. For instance, a journey map can help a business understand where it needs to loop back through the process or gracefully introduce an employee when a customer's moment of truth is not working out.

3. They enable a business to think outside of the box to create new moments of truth as new customer needs surface from the data and analytics a business collects.

4. They integrate with workflow technology to generate apps that support the processes.

In all, a journey map is a key component of any business's in-house sociology lab because the maps help the organization to understand and build the structures that customers find valuable. When well thought out they can also reduce a customer's inclination to take agency and leave a vendor for seemingly greener pastures.

Journey maps and moments of truth

The journey map for any moment of truth brings together the right people, process, and technology at the right time. If you've understood what your customers have been telling you through communities and by their uptake and use patterns, and you've modeled it in journey maps, there should be very few surprises ion your relationships. A journey map can help an organization to bring the needed resources to bear on a specific situation at the precise time that the customer makes a demand. But every process step modeled in a journey map may not require software to support it. When an app is needed a journey map can drive code generation to flesh out the application support you need for the devices that will interface with customers.

Journey maps and workflow

Workflow has the added capability of generating code to translate a journey map into running apps. For instance, a journey map might be created that analyzes and scores a customer response to an offer. Based on the score planners can determine the next best action whether that's sending a piece of content or routing the customer to sales or service or some other activity.

Perhaps a journey map defines your customer onboarding process but instead of just doing the basics like registering the user and the product, the journey map can have loops that time certain responses and then branch to other functions. So, rather than assuming a customer will start using a product a journey map might repeatedly check and escalate negative or passive responses based on the time since purchase. These actions can easily be included in workflow so that if the customer fails to onboard, a series of escalating actions could range from reminder emails to generating an alert for a customer success agent to make a phone call.

In the past, programming the detailed steps of such a workflow would take a long time and the resulting code might be hard to maintain and hard to change — two things that you do not want your customer facing business processes to become.

A business should have a journey map for all of its moments of truth and workflows for parts of journeys that involve communications with customers. Some maps can be rather complex when all the possibilities are factored in which might include looping back to a previous step or routing the customer to a live person for assistance.

Finally, the journey map is the basis for developing metrics and KPIs. The information that you diligently cull from customer data and turn into process support for moments of truth also provides the foundation for measuring your results.

The new mantra

I see a need to amend Mr. Kasparov's equation replacing weak human + machine + better process with *empowered* human + *average* computer + good software. Then we can make it the new people, process, and technology mantra. Good computing power is a commodity today and once you implement a modern application platform you can have all of the software you want to generate. But you still need to empower your people to "use good judgment" and Just F*#king Do It on behalf of customers. Empowering people might be the hardest thing we have to do in Customer Science because it might upset your business model but it's key. Our machines and software might be exceptional but in the final analysis we're still supporting people interacting with people — with empathy.

Understanding moments of truth enables us to apply technology to uncover the situations in which our resources (including people) will do the most good and technology provides the filtering and ranking needed for those deployments. The better a company gets at understanding customer moments of truth and reflecting that understanding in its customer-facing people, processes, and systems the better it will get at Customer Science.

It will also become increasingly difficult to have specialist employees who only market or only sell or only provide service since processes occur all over a company's channels and you'll need to be in all of your moments of truth. While marketing, sales, and service will remain separate departments for the foreseeable future, we should expect an amount of hybridization in the jobs. As digital marketing continues to expand, some sales jobs like renewing subscriptions are being automated. We can expect this process to accelerate as the Internet of Things continues to connect devices directly to vendors.

Analytics will play a significant role in helping to identify customers or situations into which a vendor must insert live assistance (for both sales and service). So, as Customer Science takes hold it continues to make sense for vendors to reinvest in these jobs and people, who are essential to repairing broken links in moments of truth.

Customer Science Is a Microcosm

Customer Science reflects ongoing changes throughout the global culture that have been evolving for decades. The commonality among these changes involves gathering data for analysis leading to improvements in all kinds of processes and products. *The New Yorker* business and finance columnist James Surowiecki, author of *The Wisdom of Crowds*[2], has contributed greatly to the emergence of social networking in business. His November 10, 2014, article *Better All The Time*[3] connects the importance of culturewide continuous incremental improvement using data and analytics — *kaizen* — to business and employees.

Business theorist W. Edwards Deming taught that it is far better to identify a problem in manufacturing before it manifests itself than to build a flawed product that needs to be fixed on delivery to the customer. It was a method and a message that was eagerly adopted by Japanese manufacturers and led to Japan's manufacturing dominance in the later 20th century. Statistical analysis of manufacturing data made continuous improvement possible and it forms the foundation of Customer Science.

With the adoption of statistical quality techniques, Japanese manufacturers were able to take a chunk of global manufacturing away from less rigorous American competitors. The Americans had to scramble to catch up. Today the techniques pioneered by Deming and adopted by the Japanese have become global manufacturing standards.

Not surprisingly, the approaches Deming pioneered lend themselves to many fields. As Surowiecki documents in *Better All The Time*, the same techniques have had a dramatic impact on professional and college athletes and classical concert pianists. Surowiecki points to *kaizen* as the secret to the vast performance improvement of athletes over the past few decades. Their training for events is classic *kaizen*.

Surowiecki writes that as recently as the late 1970s it was taken for granted that players arriving at the professional level had all the skills they needed and that improvement in basic skills was not likely. It was a belief that emphasized natural talent, not the ability to improve a skill or technique. For example, most players dismissed the idea of lifting weights to gain strength and mass. All this began to change when individual athletes began employing private coaches to help them gain or improve individual skills in the off-season. Today, trainers, coaches, consultants, and, yes, data analysts surround even non-professional elite athletes.

Using training data and analytics these teams can improve an individual's performance in the small-detail areas of a sport, which turns out to have big impacts on team results. Today, more pitchers than ever can throw 90 MPH (or faster) fastballs, basketball players are ambidextrous, and cyclists and distance runners have greater endurance. But more to the point, the individual performance improvements lead to greater team attainment.

By analogy, using customer data and analytics plus journey mapping and moments of truth it's now possible to apply *kaizen* strategies to front office business. Being in more moments of truth and making our customer facing processes better inevitably means that we will undergo the same incremental improvements that have penetrated most other parts of business in the last few decades.

Customer Science frames the discussion about how all this goes together. We need to adopt new processes as well as the new technologies. But we also need an overarching idea that unifies technology, people, and process because simply adding new technology to old processes won't work. Before we can succeed with new processes we must embrace one more idea, the platform.

Critical Path — The Platform

If our systems have to do more we need a new approach for building systems that is fast, accurate, precise, and that can deploy on multiple devices. This has become a requirement for any organization that expects to be competitive in markets governed by Customer Science. It describes the central importance of a software platform.

Underlying Customer Science is the software platform that supports conventional CRM databases as well as big data and analytics, journey mapping, workflow, and code generation for multiple runtime platforms. Vendors that want to implement Customer Science will first have to evaluate their platforms for suitability.

Customer Science is about data collection and its conversion into knowledge that a business can put to work in many phases of its operations. But to say that data and analytics are all we need would be a mistake. We already know that we have to put the knowledge we obtain to good use; more than ever that means providing knowledge to our employees and building it into our customer-facing automated systems from community through journey mapping and workflow and we also must build this process support into apps for a spectrum of devices from desktops to handhelds (and probably wearables).

Because knowledge requires context, which changes in the blink of an eye, our apps must also have the same flexibility to support rapidly changing customer-facing business at all levels, including the database, process, and device. If our systems are going to support the Anna Karenina Principle, they have to combine more than data and one-track workflow. They have to be able to branch to follow customers and never leave them stranded. Systems have to gracefully introduce our employees when appropriate. This means incorporating a variety of social tools, analytics, workflow, and more.

It all works together

The Anna Karenina Principle shows that moments of truth link together in cascades that must be maintained through software and authentic contact that supports customer bonding. Journey maps are the modern embodiment of the principle. Big data and analytics reveal both what the moments of truth are and show us how to measure our progress with them.

Without an organizationwide commitment to continuous improvement in the front office, results will be middling and years from now you'll still hear the old memes that CRM doesn't work or that sales people don't get anything out of SFA and that they're just collecting data for their managers. But those voices are already in the minority because some forward-looking companies are taking on continuous-improvement strategies supported by Customer Science. Those leading companies will be easy to spot because they'll be more profitable — and their customers won't say they suck.

SftC Takeaways

1. Consolidating a new science from all this.

2. What to do with all this customer data and new knowledge: building journey maps, workflows, and generating code.

3. The essential need for software platforms to support Customer Science.

Endnotes

Introduction

[1] Attributed to Wilde, Shaw, and Churchill; I thank all of them for their wit.

Chapter One

[1] Edward Wyatt, "Court Rejects Antitrust Suit in Victory for Comcast," *The New York Times*, March 27, 2013, accessed March 28, 2013, www.nytimes.com/2013/03/28/business/supreme-court-rejects-antritust-suit-against-comcast.html

[2] Susan P. Crawford, *Captive Audience: The Telecom Industry and Monopoly Power in the New Gilded Age* (New Haven: Yale University Press, 2013).

[3] Crawford, *Captive Audience* (Kindle edition. Kindle location 280-284). "A hundred years ago, the big basic-infrastructure story — the story of a network that makes other businesses possible — was the power of the railroad, a new technology that tied the country together for the first time and spurred decades of economic growth. After the completion of the first transcontinental railroad in 1869, the railroad system had mushroomed rapidly, and consolidation of independent systems by the railroad barons, chiefly J. P. Morgan, Cornelius Vanderbilt, and James J. Hill, had introduced complex new questions involving American competition and consumer protection."

[4] Wyatt, "Court Rejects Antitrust Suit in Victory for Comcast"

[5] Brown v. Allen, 344 U.S. 443

[6] "United Breaks Guitars" uploaded July 6, 2009, www.youtube.com/watch?v=5YGc4zOqozo&list=RD5YGc4zOqozo

[7] "United We Stand" uploaded March 1, 2010, www.youtube.com/watch?v=P45EouGVyeg

[8] Dave Carroll, *United Breaks Guitars: The Power of One Voice in the Age of Social Media* (New York: Hay House, Inc., 2012).

⁹ Crawford, *Captive Audience* (Kindle edition. Kindle locations 702-705). This is not completely uncommon. Lax regulatory enforcement is the price society pays sometimes for deploying new infrastructure.

¹⁰ Fred F. Reichheld, "The One Number You Need to Grow," Harvard Business Review, December 2003, hbr.org/2003/12/the-one-number-you-need-to-grow

¹¹ John Kemp, "Airlines Fly Slower to Cut Fuel Bill," Reuters, September 29, 2014, www.reuters.com/article/2014/09/29/us-airlines-fuelcells-kemp-idUSKCN0HO1ZP20140929

Chapter Two

¹ Jeremy Rifkin, *The Zero Marginal Cost Society: The Internet of Things, the Collaborative Commons, and the Eclipse of Capitalism.* (New York: Palgrave MacMillan, 2014). (Kindle edition. Kindle location 983-985).

² Rifkin, *The Zero Marginal Cost Society* (Kindle location 170).

³ Crawford, Captive Audience (Kindle edition. Kindle location 160).

Chapter Three

¹ Thomas L. Freidman, "Welcome to the 'Sharing Economy,'" *The New York Times*, July 20, 2013, www.nytimes.com/2013/07/21/opinion/sunday/friedman-welcome-to-the-sharing-economy.html?emc=eta1

Chapter Four

¹ Anna Karenina Principle, Wikipedia, http://en.wikipedia.org/wiki/Anna_Karenina_principle

² Robert D. Behn, "On the Relevance to Public Managers of: The Anna Karenina Principle," *The Behn Report*, Kennedy School of Government, 2005, http://www.ksg.harvard.edu/thebehnreport/September2005.pdf

³ Richard C. Whiteley and Diane Hessan, *Customer Centered Growth: Five Proven Strategies for Building Competitive*

Advantage (New York: The Forum Corporation, Perseus Books, 1996).

4 Nate Silver, *The Signal and the Noise: Why So Many Predictions Fail — But Some Don't* (New York: Penguin Group U.S., 2012). p. 13. (Kindle edition 2012-09-27).

Chapter Five

1 Garry Kasparov, "The Chess Master and the Computer," *The New York Review of Books,* February 11, 2010, http://www.nybooks.com/articles/archives/2010/feb/11/the-chess-master-and-the-computer/

2 Erik Brynjolfsson and Andrew McAfee, *Race Against the Machine: How the Digital Revolution is Accelerating Innovation, Driving Productivity, and Irreversibly Transforming Employment and the Economy* (Digital Frontier Press. Kindle edition. Kindle locations 808-809) and *The Second Machine Age: Work, Progress, and Prosperity in a Time of Brilliant Technologies* (W. W. Norton & Company. Kindle edition. Kindle location 710-711).

3 Dharmesh Shah and Brian Halligan, *Inbound Marketing: Get Found Using Google, Social Media, and Blogs* (Hoboken, New Jersey: John Wiley & Sons, Inc., revised and updated 2014).

4 OnStartups.com

5Culture Code: Creating A Lovable Company: An inside peek at how we work and what we believe at HubSpot. http://www.slideshare.net/HubSpot/the-hubspot-culture-code-creating-a-company-we-love?utm_source=slideshow02&utm_medium=ssemail&utm_ca mpaign=share_slideshow_loggedout

Chapter Six

1 Perhaps in the future large enterprises might have sociology teams just as they now have sales, marketing, service, engineering and many other teams. As sociology — and not just product marketing — becomes a larger part of a company's approach to the marketplace, dividing outbound marketing from inbound sociology might make a good deal of sense.

[2] "The State of Salesforce," 2013-2014, page 17.

Chapter Nine

[1] Nate Silver, *The Signal and the Noise: Why So Many Predictions Fail — But Some Don't* (New York: Penguin Group U.S., 2012). p. 13. (Kindle edition 2012-09-27).

[2] Julie Wittes Schlack,

http://blog.communispace.com/connect/deriving-maximum-impact-from-online-communities/

Wittes Schlack is one of the founding members of Communispace Corporation. She has been instrumental in designing and continually evolving Communispace's online community offering. As SVP of innovation and design, she leads an innovation and research group whose dual mission is to uncover new patterns and trends in online community behavior and to test new techniques and technologies for engaging people in online communities and social networks. Her group's work has been widely published and it has transformed Communispace's ability to help companies hardwire the voice of the customer into their businesses.

[3] Diane Hessan, "4 Essential Ingredients in Consumer Storytelling," Inc.com, December 13, 2013, http://www.inc.com/4-essential-ingredients-in-consumer-storytelling.html

Chapter Ten

[1] Click https://www.youtube.com/watch?v=7xb2eIiVNQg to see a video on this application.

Chapter Eleven

[1] Thomas S. Kuhn, *The Structure of Scientific Revolutions* (Chicago: University of Chicago Press. 50th Anniversary Edition, p. 10. (Kindle edition. Kindle location 782).

Kuhn distinguishes between normal science, which is a science as we know it, and the period before it is established. Before a science is established there is a chaotic period in which people speculate about nature. The best speculators devise questions that can be formulated as experiments that can prove or disprove the general nature of a science. Often math is involved and used to accumulate evidence of the proofs. Those proofs are gradually consolidated into the framework of a science that can then be used to identify questions that can be studied with the concepts developed from the new science, and those that lie outside of the framework. What happens after the consolidation is normal science. In the front office we have undergone a long period of hypothesis and experimentation that has led to this moment when we can declare the existence of Customer Science.

[2] James Surowiecki, *The Wisdom of Crowds* (New York: Random House, 2004)

[3] Surowiecki, "Better All The Time," *The New Yorker*, November 10, 2014
http://www.newyorker.com/magazine/2014/11/10/better-time

Acknowledgements

Most people have never heard of analyst relations (AR), a vital function in technology companies. Much like public relations, which seeks to keep communications open between various constituents like the press, customers, and other entities, the AR function is designed to reach out to a company's key market influencers. The analysts that pass judgment on technology companies routinely interact with AR teams, often getting confidential information on new developments in advance of the general market so that they can write about them.

AR succeeds or fails based on the talent and hard work of the people who staff the department, and they have a tough job. They're a rare breed, part technologist, part business maven; they're diplomats, facilitators, negotiators, psychologists, and more. Without them, I have serious reservations about whether the tech sector would be what it is today.

I've always been fortunate to work with highly skilled and hard-working AR staffers to get a story about a new product, access a valued customer, or just to understand a company's direction. There were many AR people involved in helping me get interviews for this book, both within their respective companies and with their most precious assets — their end customers. I offer them my thanks and by extension, I thank all the AR people who have helped me over my long analyst career.

One of the differences between a self-published book and one put out by a traditional publishing house is the level of attention given to editing. Often, self-publishers like me produce their volumes without the assistance of a professional editor and very often it shows. I am grateful to Alison C. Lowander for her fine efforts to edit this book. (All the remaining mistakes are mine.) Along the way I learned many valuable things about writing, editing, and publishing, and I wouldn't trade the experience for anything.

My old and good friend, Paul Greenberg, author of *CRM at the Speed of Light*, read the early *Solve for the Customer* manuscript and provided wonderful feedback. So did Anthony Lye, president and CEO of Red Book Connect, who is also a good friend, a major influence in the industry, and whose judgments I trust implicitly. John Taschek, SVP, Strategy at salesforce.com, has been a friend for a long time and he performed yeoman's service reviewing and providing feedback.

For more than 10 years Diane Hessan, CEO, Startup Institute and chairman of Communispace Corporation, has graciously given her time to educate me on the finer points of social networking and community building. Many thanks to her. Chris Selland, VP, business development at HP Software, Big Data, has been a colleague in the Enterprise Irregulars for a long time. He shared his insights about community and provided access to Jason Bailey, senior manager of digital marketing, and Danielle Sandahl, global campaigns manager at HP Vertica. Lori Jenkins, now a Customer Success Manager at Optimizely, was responsible for managing the successful implementation of Get Satisfaction at HP Vertica, and provided me with great detail on the process. Thanks also to Erling Amundson, senior manager social insights, Symantec Corporation. Ken Grady, CIO, New England BioLabs, Inc., was intimately involved in architecting the new freezer program at NEB; he provided the details and graciously reviewed my copy. Dharmesh Shah, CTO at HubSpot, provided great background information and insights into managing people in a modern business. Bluewolf CEO Eric Berridge shared an interesting perspective on the future of CRM. Tien Tzuo, cofounder and CEO of Zuora, and I go way back. He introduced me to the subscription revolution and was an important factor in my education about subscriptions.

Jim Dickie, a managing principal of CSO Insights, has been researching selling, the sales process, and sales management with his partner Barry Traylor for more than 20 years. Jim generously shared his research with me and provided insight into how businesses use CRM and SFA. Wendy Lea, CEO at Cintrifuse and chair of the board at Get Satisfaction; Alan Trefler, CEO at Pegasystems; and Mark Woolen, SVP, product marketing Sales Cloud at Salesforce.com, all provided insights and background information during the research phase.

Thanks also to my colleagues in the CRM–influencer community who were supportive of my effort in writing *Solve for the Customer*. Your friendship and insights make this job fun.

CPSIA information can be obtained at www.ICGtesting.com
Printed in the USA
LVOW07s1152250315

431918LV00057B/840/P